Magic
With
Cards

Magic With Cards

♠♣♥♦ 113 Easy-to-Perform Miracles
With an Ordinary Deck of Cards

**Frank Garcia
and George Schindler**

Illustrations by Ed Tricomi

BARNES
&NOBLE
BOOKS
NEW YORK

This edition published by Barnes & Noble, Inc.,
by arrangement with Frank Garcia and George Schindler.

1993 Barnes & Noble Books

ISBN 1-56619-124-6

Printed and bound in the United States of America
M 9 8 7 6 5

For Lillian and Nina—
the women in our lives

Contents

Magic
With
Cards

Foreword

The rapidly growing interest in magic as a hobby prompted the writing of this book at this time. Having been professional magicians for the better part of our lives we know that card tricks are the most popular tricks in magic. They are easily performed anywhere you go and always bring a great and satisfying response. The new magician should learn to present his or her tricks properly without being hampered by technical terms, intricate sleights, and manipulations. That is not to say that you should not learn more advanced forms of the art. But when you begin you should have some basic, easy-to-do effects for openers.

Concentrate on these for handling, patter, and presentation. Your magic must be entertaining above everything else. Without entertainment, magic is simply a puzzle and can be very boring to watch. We have included the patter (the things to say) used in your performance. Use it in the beginning, but later on you'll find that you will develop your own presentation and your own words.

Although the tricks are easy to perform, we feel that we must caution you to practice carefully before presenting them. Magic must be kept secret or you lose the mystery. The worst exposer of magic is the unprepared performer. *Never reveal the secret of your trick.* You will often be tempted to show others how clever you are, but you must not succumb to that temptation. While you are performing your audience will have great respect for your talents; once the trick is revealed the respect is gone and the magic is lost. Should someone ask you how a trick is done, you can answer: "Very quickly" or "Very well!"

In keeping with the secrecy of magic, *never repeat a trick for the same audience.* To be most effective, magic must encompass the element of surprise. If your audience knows what is coming, they'll know what to look for. Your misdirection is lost.

The material in this book has been selected from hundreds of tried and tested effects. We have tried to collect the best principles available, putting them into modern dress for the modern magician. Many time-worn tricks are still workable in their new clothes. We selected commercial and audience-appealing material. Most of the card tricks you see have been developed over the years by ourselves and other members of the magical fraternity whose devotion to the art is deep and passionate. The origins of the principles are, for the most part, unknown. The variations are myriad and never ending. These are the best of the best.

We have tried to offer the basics in several forms. A "pick-a-card" trick is broken into two components—the location (how to find the card) and the revelation (how to reveal it). Most of these are interchangeable so that you can use one location and another revelation for the final effect. Use some imagination and you will create new tricks by combining the various principles. Vary your material so that you are not using too many of the same locations each time. Adding two or three tricks in a logical sequence will help you develop routines. And for magic's sake, don't do too many at one sitting! There is nothing worse than someone doing cards tricks to excess.

After you have mastered some of the miracles in this work,

we urge you to go further with the art and learn some sleight-of-hand. The professional magicians you see on the stage and on television all do their locations with "hand magic." To introduce you to' the basics of better card handling we have included a chapter in this book on the shuffles and controls that are the rudiments you will need when you decide you're ready. You will always look better when you learn how to handle the deck. You will also have a better understanding and appreciation for the professional magician.

We wish to thank the devotees of card magic throughout the years who have invented, developed, and polished the principles and effects used here. We have taken these gems and added our own touches in patter, presentation, and creating routines. Special thanks to Bob Reiss of Reiss Games for his suggestions and encouragement during the writing of this book. We hope you will enjoy it. Get yourself a deck of cards—and have fun.

Frank Garcia
George Schindler

Playing Cards — A Brief History

The origin of playing cards is obscure. No one really knows who invented them or when it happened. When the origin of something is unknown it is often the custom to attribute it to the Devil or Asia. To this day playing cards are still known as the "Devil's playthings."

Playing cards probably originated in Hindustan about A.D. 800. In an ancient Chinese dictionary, Ching-tsze-tung (1678), it is said that cards were invented during the reign of Seun-Ho (A.D. 1120). He was supposed to have used them to entertain his concubines. In ancient Egypt they were said to have been used for religious purposes. There are references in India that claim the Brahmans invented the card.

Modern playing cards were first mentioned in Italy in 1279. The European playing card is the closest thing to our present day card. Playing cards first appeared in Germany, then France, and then Spain. A painter named Gringonneur designed special cards for King Charles VI of France. Charles Poupart (treasurer of King Charles's household) made an entry in his account book in 1392 which describes the purchase:

> To Jacquemin Gringonneur, painter, for three packs of cards in gold and divers colours of several designs, for the King for his diversion.

A Franciscan friar in 1493 decided that playing cards were indeed "invented by the Devil." We can safely say that playing cards are well over 700 years old.

The earliest known playing cards were called the "Tarot" or "Tarocchini" and consisted of between sixty and eighty cards in the pack. There were four suits with picture cards denoting members of the royalty. They were only used by the royalty since they were quite expensive. The suits were much like present-day cards. In Italy and Spain they used cups similar to our Hearts. Their Spades were depicted as swords; money, where we use Diamonds, and batons that were similar to our Clubs. The Germanic nations had suits like Hearts, Acorns (Spades), Bells (instead of our Diamonds), and Leaves (perhaps related to our Clubs). The French used the *Trefle* or trefoil clover to represent Clubs.

Early cards were sometimes round in shape. Our modern rectangular cards evolved around 1500 and depicted Kings, Queens, and Knaves as court cards. In England, as early as 1526 King Henry VIII proclaimed that playing cards were to be outlawed, along with "Tables, Dice and Bowls." In 1541 a statute was passed to allow the game to the working man only at Christmastide.

Since the sixteenth century magicians have used playing cards to entertain and mystify audiences. Reginald Scott describes card tricks in his *Discouverie of Witchcraft* published in 1584. Early card magicians were called "jugglers." Gamblers prior to the eighteenth century used marked cards and card location systems for cheating. Many of these old methods are employed for card handling today.

Modern magicians since Robert-Houdin have been using cards for entertainment. In the early 1920s Howard Thurston made cards vanish and leap through the air. Even Harry Houdini, most famous as an escape artist, was first billed as the "King of Cards."

Card magicians became more and more popular in recent years. Vaudeville stars such as Cardini brought playing cards to the stage.

Card tricks are the most popular tricks in all of magic. They can be done on stage and in your living room. They do not require large vans to carry them or assistants to help work them. Playing cards are found everywhere you go. And now — let's learn!

The Key Card

♠♣♥♦ Hundreds of years ago, playing cards were valuable objects used only by the rich. The earliest card tricks did not employ sleight-of-hand techniques common today, but they did use the "key card" principle.

The "Key Card" Principle

If you know the name of one card in the deck and place this card next to an "unknown" card you can always find the unknown card, no matter how often deck may be cut. The "known" card is called the "key." It is the key to finding the unknown card. Here is a simple trick that uses the "key."

Fingerprints Never Lie

After your spectator has thoroughly shuffled the cards, have him select any one and remove it from the deck. Turn your back after he has taken his card. *"I'll turn my back so that I can't see the card. What I'd like you to do is to press your thumb on the face of the deck so that your fingerprint will be in the center of the card."* While the spectator is doing this, secretly look at the bottom card of your pack. This will be your key card, so remember it. Turn back to the spectator when he has finished. *"Don't let me see the card."* Place the deck face down on the table. *"Please put your card on top of the deck. Now cut the deck and replace the cut so that your fingerprint-card is in the center of the pack. There is no way I have of knowing where your card lies at present. In recent years, the art of fingerprinting has been developed to such a fine degree that it is possible to identify a person in minutes by looking at one of his prints. I will attempt to find your card by combining a bit of magic with modern police techniques. May I see your thumb, the one you used to identify your card? Thank you. You can see the lines and whorls, and as amazing as it may seem, no two people have the same prints."*

Turn the deck face up on the table and spread the cards ribbon-fashion so that you can see all of them. The card immediately to the right of the "key" card is the one the spectator chose. You can use a magnifying glass or someone's eyeglasses to help you perform the trick.

"I'll need some magnification for this one. May I borrow your glasses?" You already know the card, but now we need some acting ability for the magic. Pretend to look at each card through the glass, sifting them one by one, supposedly look-

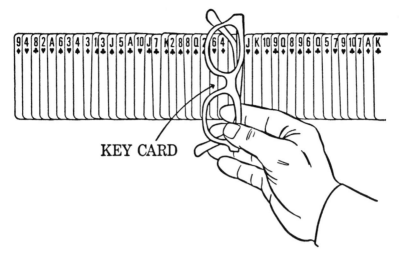

KEY CARD

ing for the fingerprint. Find the selected card and push it forward. *"May I look at your thumb again, please? Ah yes! This is the one. Here is your card, sir, with your very own fingerprint in the center."*

Tell the Truth

The bottom card will be your key card here. Spread the cards ribbon style across the table. *"Take any card you like, please. Do you want to change your mind? Please look at the card and remember it."* Once the card is removed, scoop up the cards again and cut the pack in half. Point to the top card of the half containing your key. *"Please put your card here in the middle of the deck."* Cut that pack in half so that the key is on top of the selected card. Hand the pack to the spectator.

"Let's play a little game. I'll turn my back and you will deal the cards onto the table one at a time. As you do, tell me the name of the card. When you come to your card, call it by a different name. In other words, tell me the truth each time— except when you come to your card. I will try to determine when you are lying by listening to the sound of your voice."

Have the spectator follow the steps. The card he will call *after* the key card is the selected card. You will merely listen for the key and when he mis-names the selected card, you shout at him dramatically: *"THAT'S A LIE!"*

Note: If you casually look through the cards before handing him the pack, you can actually see his card. In that case you can announce: *"That's a lie—your card is the Six of Spades"* (or whatever it is).

Royal Mounties

Your key card is on the bottom of the deck. Allow the spectator to select a card and to replace it on top of the deck. You cut the deck, placing the key directly on top of his card.

"There is an old story about the Canadian Mounted Police, who boast that they always get their man. This deck has two Kings who are actually retired 'Mounties.' Please remember the name of your card while I find my policemen." Turn the deck with faces toward you. Spread the cards, looking for the Kings. Actually you are looking for your key card, which you cut to the bottom of the deck. The selected card will now be the top card of the pack. Go through the cards again and remove the two black Kings (Clubs and Spades). Place these on the table, face up.

"Here they are—Fred and Peter of the Royal Mounted Police. I'm going to put them into the middle of the deck, face up." Place the deck behind your back. Pick up the first King and place it face up under the top card of the deck. Pick up the second King and put it face up on top of the deck. Cut the pack.

"The two boys are now in the deck and hopefully they're hard at work looking for their man. What was the name of your card, please?" After the card has been named, place the deck on the table and ribbon-spread the cards. The two Kings will be face up in the middle, with the selected card face down between them. Have the spectator look at the card. *"I guess the tale is true—the Mounties always get their man."*

From the Pocket

After having the deck shuffled, glimpse the bottom card as your key. Start to deal the cards onto the table, one at a time.

"As I deal, please stop me at any time you choose." Deal the cards until he stops you. *"Right here? If you like I'll go further."* If he wants you to deal a few more, do so. If not, stop where he asks. *"Please look at the last card I dealt and remember it."* After this has been done he is to replace the card on top of the others on the table. You add your pack to the top and hand him the deck for a few cuts. You have now set the key above his card. Pick up the deck once more. *"Let me remove the Joker. . . ."* Pretend to look for the Joker, but actually find the selected card next to the key and cut it to the top. If the deck has a Joker, remove it and leave it on the table. If not, merely comment that you have no Joker. Place the deck in your right-hand pants pocket, so that the backs are facing away from your body. Involve a second spectator. *"Do you know what card this man has chosen? Do you know where to find it? It's in my pocket with the rest of the cards. Very quickly reach into my pocket and pull out any card."* Due to the fact there is very little room for a hand in the pocket, the spectator will pull out the top card. Ask them both to name the card and show it to your audience. *"I'm glad you took only the card. I also have a ten-dollar bill in that pocket."* Remove the cards and turn your pockets inside out to show they are empty. Kid the second spectator: *"You may keep the ten dollars for your work in assisting me."*

On Command

For this location the deck is shuffled and spread on the table, face up. *"While my back is turned, please turn one card face down. Remember this card but do not let me see the face."* Turn your back so he can follow your instructions. Now turn back and scoop up all the cards on the table. The bottom card is easily seen as your key. Turn the deck face down and request that the selected card be placed on top. *"Cut the deck."* You are now ready for the revelation. *"As I look through the cards, please concentrate on the card you selected."* Go through the cards, their faces toward you. Find the key. This time count back so that the selected card is fourth from the top when you cut the deck. Place the deck on the table. *"I can't seem to locate your card. Perhaps I can cause it to move out of the deck at my command. Keep your eyes on the deck. What is the name of your card please?"* He will name it. Let us say, for example, that he selected the Six of Spades. *"Six of Spades—Come forth!"* Watch the deck as though something is about to move. Be mysterious. *"SIX OF SPADES, COME FORTH!"* Command it. *"Ah, there it is!"* The spectator will insist that nothing has happened. *"The Six of Spades did in fact come forth. Look."* Count the cards off the top of the deck. *"Here's the first, the second, and the third. The Six of Spades comes fourth."* Turn over the fourth card and laugh with the rest of the crowd, unless of course they jeer at a corny but funny gag.

The Pulse Trick

For the previous tricks we were using a key card on the bottom of the pack. The key can also be used on top of the deck. Here is a surprising effect where the top card is known. You can merely look at it when going through the cards to see if it's a full deck. The deck is placed on top of a drinking glass so that it is seen by the group. Pick a spectator from the group.

"Did you know that playing cards are very sensitive to body vibrations? Let me try an experiment that is most unusual. Cut a small packet of cards from the top of the deck and hold them to your heart. Make sure we don't see the faces of any of the cards."

Allow the spectator to follow your instructions. *"What you are doing is picking up your heartbeat. The vibrations are hitting the card closest to your body. Please look at that card for a moment and remember it. Now cut the small packet in half and complete your cut so the vibrations are in the center of the packet."* Have another spectator lift up some of the cards that remain on the glass. The first spectator is instructed to place his cards on top of the cards on the glass. The second spectator will now add his cards to the pack, losing the selected card in the center.

Pick up the cards and turn them face up on the table, spreading them across the table so that most of them are seen. The selected card will be directly to the *left* of the key card. Go back to the original spectator. *"Please point your index finger. Fine. Now I will hold your pulse and I will pass your hand over the pack. You will point to the cards as we pass them. Your pulse rate should match the vibrations coming off the card you chose."* At this point start at one end and move his or her hand across the spread of cards on the table. Pretend to pass it and go back a few times, and finally push the spectator's hand forward so that the index finger lands on the selected card. *"This must be the card; it's beating exactly like your pulse!"*

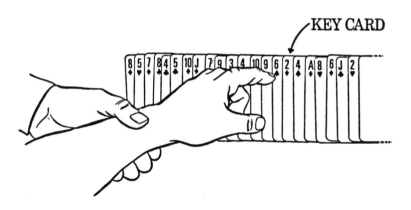

KEY CARD

Marked

The presentation of the trick is most times more important than the method by which the trick is accomplished. Here is a perfect example of proper presentation.

Your key card is on the bottom of the pack. Spread the cards on the table, face down.

"Sir, I'd like you to choose any card you wish. Neither one of us will see the face of the card. Please pull one card out of the spread." After he has done this, put the cards together and request that he place his card on top of the deck, *"without looking at it."* Offer him a soft pencil or pen. *"Please initial or mark the back of this card with some identifying symbol, so we can recognize it again."* This having being done, ask him to cut the deck *". . . to lose the card in the middle."*

Pick up the deck and turn it face up, spreading it ribbon-fashion across the table. You will spot your known key card. The card directly to its right is the selected card, which the spectator has not yet seen.

Hand him the pen or pencil so that the point is facing down toward the table. *"Please hold this pencil between your thumb and forefinger. I will hold your wrist and we will pass the point across the tops of the cards."* Begin at one end of the spread and slowly move his wrist across the faces of the cards. *"You have no idea which of these cards is the one you marked, is that correct, sir?"* He will acknowledge that he doesn't. As you come over the selected card, apply slight pressure to his wrist in a downward direction. *"Did you feel something just then?"* No matter what he replies, you push the hand down so that the pencil touches the selected card. *"Something directed you to that card. Please turn it over and see if it bears your mark. It does!"*

Get-Together

Allow your spectator to shuffle the deck and cut it in half. He will give you one half, keeping the other half for himself. *"We will each shuffle our cards to mix them thoroughly."* Each of you does this. *"We will each take out one card, look at it, and remember it."* Pull a card from the center of your half, pretend to look at it and put it on top of your pile. Actually you will peek at your own bottom card, and remember it. *"Place the card you selected on top of the pack."*

At this point add the cards in your hand to the top of his

cards. This puts your key card on top of his card. Ask him to cut the deck a few times *". . . to lose both cards in the deck."*

"My card was the [name the bottom key card]. *What was yours?"* After he names his card, say: *"I will now perform a bit of magic without touching the cards in your hand. I will send my card to meet yours. They are now together in the pack. Please look through the cards and verify that I have accomplished this amazing feat."*

Wanna Bet?

This one is good for laughs, as well as being an amazing discovery of a selected card. The key card is on the bottom of the deck. Ask the spectator to cut the deck into three even piles. He will now take a card from the middle of any pile, and after looking at it will replace it on top of any other pile. You now put all the piles together, making sure that the key card will go on top of the selected card. (In case he puts the card on top of the pile containing the key, ask him to cut the pile and replace the cut. (This will do they same thing—putting the key on the selected card.)

Turn the pack face up. Cut it into three heaps. Spread each heap to show the spectator all the cards. *"Please tell me which group contains your card."* After the spectator has done this, pick up the group he selected. By this time you have seen your key card. You know that the very next card is the selected card. Turn the packet face down and start to deal the cards face up onto the table, overlapping each card. Deal them slowly, so that you can be sure that every card is seen. As soon as you deal your key card you know the next card is the one he has selected. Deal this onto the table along with the others. Then deal two more cards and stop. *"I'll make you a bet that the next card I turn over will be your card."* Naturally, since the spectator saw you pass his card, he will assume that you missed it. He will take the bet. At this moment, pick up his card and turn it face down. To avoid arguments don't make this a real money bet. The trick is just for fun.

Reversed

Hold the deck in your left hand. Push the cards to your right, using your left thumb to push and the right thumb to pull the cards into your right hand. Move the deck forward toward the spectator and ask him or her to remove any card. Once this has been done, square the pack by hitting it on the edge of the table. In this way you can get a glimpse of the bottom card. This is your key. The deck is held squarely in the left hand. (See illustration below.) The right thumb and middle fingers grab the bottom half and pull the cards away from the deck. For future reference, this is called the "key cut."

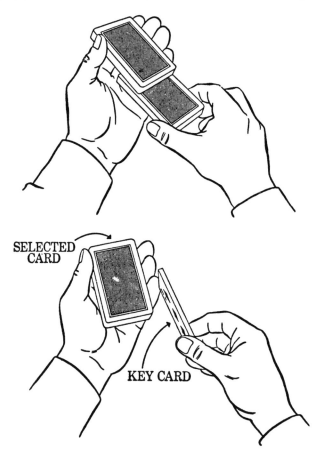

SELECTED CARD

KEY CARD

The spectator will now place his selected card on top of the half in your left hand. Add the cards from your right hand and the deck is complete again, with the key card on top of the selected card.

"Please take the deck and cut it several times so as to lose the card you selected." Take the deck back after it has been cut a few times. (The cutting will not disturb the key.) Turn the cards face up and look through them, fanning them as you did at the beginning of the trick. *"As you can see, your card is lost among these."* You are really looking for your key card. When you come to it, cut the deck at that point. This brings the key to the bottom and the selected card to the top of the deck. Place the deck behind your back.

"I will attempt to find your card without looking at the deck."

Behind your back you will take the top card, turn it upside down and insert it somewhere in the middle of the deck. Now bring out any card and drop it on the table. *"Is this your card?"* Wrong! Remove another card from the bottom. *"How about this one?"* Wrong again. Bring the deck in front of you and place it face down on the table. *"It seems I can't find the card without looking. But perhaps I can make a magical pass and cause your card to jump into the air."* Make a magical pass over the cards. *"Did you see it jump? You didn't? Why it jumped right out, turned itself over, and slipped back into the deck."*

Spread the cards across the table and reveal the single card inverted (face up) in the pack.

A Quick Year

We have an unusual location trick here. The key card finds the selected card and puts it in the right place.

Reverse the bottom card of your deck. Spread the cards for a selection and use the key cut so that the key will be on top of the selected card.

"Your card is lost in the pack, as you can see." Spread the cards. Feign surprise as you see a reversed card. Cut the deck at that point so that the reversed card is on top. Turn it over. (The selected card is now second from the top.) *"How many weeks in the year?"* The answer is naturally "fifty-two." Deal down a pile of five cards and then a smaller pile with only two cards. *"Five and two."* Pick up the two cards, add them to the five and place them all back on top of the

deck. *"How many months in the year?"* The reply is "twelve," so you deal twelve cards onto the table. Pick them up and place them back on top of the deck. *"How many days in a week?"* Deal seven cards and put them back on top of the deck. Put the deck on the table. *"What time is it?"* Don't wait for an answer. *"It's time to find your card. What was the name of the card?"* On hearing the reply turn the top card face up. It will be the selected card.

In Between

Two spectators are better than one. This is called audience participation, and it will make your act look bigger. Have each select a card. The same key card can find them both. Merely have them replaced in the pack, one on top of the other. Do the key cut to place the key card on top of the selected cards and you're ready for a fine unusual discovery.

"Will anyone in the audience please call out the name of any card in the deck? Not one of the chosen cards, please." When the card has been named, ask that person to come up to help you. Turn the pack face up and look for the card that was just called. You are also looking for your key card. Cut the pack so that one selected card is on top and the other on the bottom of the deck. Hand the card to the third spectator, the one who named a card.

"This is the card you called out. Please turn it face up and place it in the center of the pack." Cut the cards exactly as you did for the key cut. Allow this spectator to put the card on top of the half in your left hand. The right hand section is on top of this and you have placed his or her card between the two selected cards. *"I'm glad you came today. You have found our missing cards."* Ask the first two spectators to name their cards. Ribbon-spread the deck. The card on either side of the face-up card will be shown and the trick has been completed successfully.

Blindfolded Location

This is an unusual use of the key-card principle. It is preferable to use your own deck. Remove the Ten of Diamonds. Take a straight pin and prick a small hole just above the zero of the 10 at the left index corner of the card. Do the same on the other side, turning the card around. The small bump will hardly be noticed, but you will be able to feel it with your thumb on the back of the card. Place this key card so that it lies tenth from the bottom of the deck. You are now ready to present a most unusual effect.

Spread the cards for the selection of a card. Make sure that only the top half is offered so that he does not select any of the bottom ten cards. Undercut the deck as you did for the key cut and have the selected card replaced on top of the cards in your left hand. Add the right-hand cards to this and your selected card is now eleven cards away from the key.

"I will now find your card while totally in the dark." Request that someone blindfold you with a hankerchief. The cards are kept in your left hand as this is done. Now deal the cards onto the table one at a time. When you reach the key card you will actually feel it with the right thumb. Deal this onto the table face up. *"Is this the card you chose?"* The answer will be *"No."* *"What card is this one, please?"* Someone will tell you it's a Ten. *"Of course not. That's my indicator. Please count ten more cards and look at the tenth card."* It will be the selected card. Remove the blindfold.

Magic 12

This is a method of making any card a permanent key. The key is a single card, which you will mark as you perform this effect.

Allow the spectator to remove any twelve cards from the pack. As he is shuffling these, you will take the balance of the deck and nick the top of the top card with your fingernail. Turn the deck around and do the same with the other side. Do not be too obvious. A small nick will mark the card for you.

Place the deck on the table. Your key is on top. *"Please place any number of your cards in your pocket. It makes no difference how many. Shuffle the rest of the cards and look at the one on the bottom. Remember this card. Please place all your cards on top of the deck."* Pick up the deck and hand it to him. *"Please deal out a row of six cards. Overlap them as you deal."* When this has been finished, announce: *"I think we'll need another six."* While he is dealing, you are watching for the key card. As soon as you see it, start to count—counting the key as number "one." The amount of cards he deals from there is the same as the number in his pocket. If you have started with number one, the last number you counted is the one you need. Looking at the spread on the table, you can also tell that the selected card is the one that was dealt immediately before the nicked card. Having this information, you are now ready to proceed.

"Please put your finger on one of the cards in the middle of the row on the table." If he puts his finger on the selected

card you have a miracle. You will then tell him how many cards he has in his pocket and allow him to turn the card face up for a surprise. This will happen once in a while. He will probably select one of the other cards. *"Keep your finger on that card for a moment, please."* Pick up the other cards on the table, making sure the selected card is on the bottom of the packet. As you place the packet on the rest of the deck, get a peek at this card. You must know what it is.

"May I see the card under your finger?" Pick up the card. *"This card is a Seven"* (or whatever it is). *"Let me think for a moment."* Mutter to yourself, allowing them to hear you. *"Let's see. Seven from fifteen is eight, divided by six. . . ."* Speak up firmly now. *"You should have four cards in your pocket."* Name the correct amount. *"Please count them."* Study the card in your hand for a moment. Mumble again. *"Eight and six is fourteen Diamonds, times three, divided by seven."* Louder. *"Your card is the Jack of Clubs"* (or whatever it is). *"See how it pays to know your numbers? Sometimes I'm sorry I failed Arithmetic."*

A Trick from Down Under

When the spectator has a chance to find his or her own card, without the possibility of the magician's manipulations, the trick is usually more effective. This one also uses the key card.

Have three, four, or five spectators each select cards at random from a shuffled pack. You note the bottom card as your key when they replace the cards. Have the last person replace his card first, then the next to last, etc. Cut the deck after all of them have placed their cards on top of the pack. You have apparently lost the cards in the center. Turn the deck face up, look for your key, and cut it to the bottom. Let us assume that four people have each selected cards.

"You have each selected a card and I shall attempt to find it with the Australian deal. You look surprised. I suppose you'll tell me that you never heard of the Australian deal? You haven't? Well, let's see what we can do to demonstrate it." Turn the pack face up. Deal one card to each of the four spectators, but turn it face down as you set it in front him or her. Now turn the pack face down and deal one more card to

each person. (These are the selected cards.) Continue to deal four more cards, one at a time, until each spectator has a pile of six cards.

"Please pick up your cards and we will all do the Australian deal." You do the same thing you instruct them to do, but use the pack in your hands. *"The top card goes under the pile. The next card is dealt onto the table. Got it? Good. One more down under, the next one on the table. This is how the deal got its name. The next card goes down under."*

Allow the spectators to continue to deal this way until only one card will remain in each person's hand. *"If the Australian down-under deal was done correctly, you will each hold the card you originally selected a while ago."*

Too Tired

Your key here is an entire block of ten cards, all of the same suit. For example, we will use the ten Clubs, arranged from Ace to Ten. These are in sequence, with the Ace on the bottom of the stack. The entire group is placed on the bottom of the deck before you begin the trick. The cards can be arranged this way in the card case. Do this as your first trick.

"I've been doing card tricks all day and I'm so tired. But I would like to do one for you. Perhaps you can do the trick and I'll just tell you what to do. Boy, am I tired! Here's a pack of cards. Please take the cards out of the case and set them on the table, face down in front of you."

Have the spectator do all the work. *"Take a card out of the middle of the deck and look at it. Please remember it and put it on top of the pack. Fine. Now cut the deck so it's lost in the middle. Turn the pack face up, please. Cut the deck once more."*

You will now instruct the spectator to cut the deck and re-place the cut as many times as is necessary, until you see one of the ten clubs on the face of the pack. At that point you stop him. Let us assume that the Nine of Clubs is on the face of the deck. This will indicate to you that the selected card is nine cards from the top of the deck. Have him turn the deck face down and put his finger on the cards.

"Place your finger on top of the deck. Your card is . . . let me see . . .". (pause) *"twenty-two cards down."* Pause for a moment and he will lift his finger. *"Hold it! You moved your finger! Put it back. When you moved the finger the card traveled further up. It's now the ninth card down. Please lift your finger and count, face down, nine cards. Is that your card? Thanks for the help. I've rested up a bit and now I'll show you a few more miracles."* The selected card will always appear at the position indicated by the Club. Do your next trick.

Four Keys

This interesting presentation requires four key cards. To make them easier to remember, we will use Fours. Place the Fours on top of the deck before you begin the trick. You will also have to practice a simple bit of business with a blindfold. If you take a large handkerchief and have someone blindfold you, you will find that you can see down through the spaces around your nose. If the blindfold is straight across your eyes you merely lift your head back a bit and your vision is quite

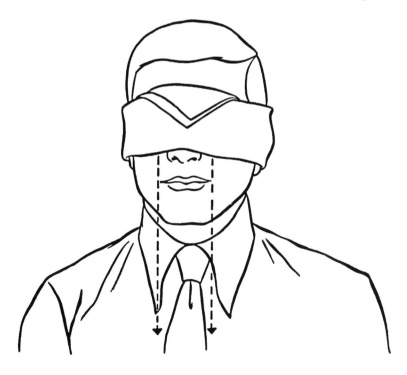

good. Using this principle, we are ready to begin a reputation-making "miracle."

Hand the deck to the first of four spectators. *"Please deal four cards in a row onto the table. Now deal the rest of the cards into four piles until you run out of cards."* (The Fours are now on the bottom of each of the four piles.) Have each spectator take a single card from the middle of each of one of the piles. They are told to remember these cards and place them on top of their respective packets. They will now cut the packets in half and complete the cuts. One of the spectators will now put all the piles together into a single pack. Take the deck, turn it face up on the table in front of you, and spread the cards so that they are all seen. Now have one of the four spectators blindfold you. Move up close to the table so that you are in a position to see down through the opening. You should be able to see all the cards. Pretend to have difficulty moving about. Pass your hand over the spread. *"Am I near the cards, please?"* Look for each of the Fours. The card immediately to the right of each Four is a selected card. Spot the first selected card at your left. Let us say for example it is the Nine of Clubs. Build up the effect. *"If each of you will please concentrate on the card you selected, I will try to pick up your thoughts. I have the vibrations of a black card. I believe one of you selected a Club. It is a Ten . . . no, I think it is a Nine of Clubs. Am I correct?"* Do the same with the second and third cards. *"I get the impression of a picture card. Someone is thinking of the Jack of Diamonds. I feel a strange sensation. It is a Seven of Spades. . . ."* For the last card you will pass your hand over the cards touching them lightly as you pass. Finally your hand will settle on the last selected card. Pick it up. *"This card has a strange aura. Is this the card you chose?"* Remove the blindfold, closing your eyes very tightly as you do. Open your eyes and blink them as though trying to get used to the light. *"This has been a very trying experience. Please don't think of anything for a few moments, so I can recover my senses."*

The buildup of this effect is most important.

In My Mind's Eye

You can also be blindfolded in performing this one, which also uses four keys. This time your key cards are in pairs. Set the deck with four Threes on the bottom of the deck and four Fives on the top. We are using these particular cards since they are not prominent or obvious pairs, such as picture cards or Aces. Hand the deck to the spectator.

"Please deal four piles of cards, dealing from left to right."

When this has been completed he will have a five on the bottom of each pile and a three on top.

"Take a card from the middle of any pile, remember it, and place it on top of any of those piles. Now cover that card with one of the piles. Put the whole works on top of another pile. Put the last two piles together. Give the deck a cut. You must admit your card is now hopelessly lost." Have yourself blindfolded or, if this isn't possible, sit with your back to the audience. *"I'll turn around. You'll probably be glad to see me back. Then again . . . you may not after that joke!"*

When you are all set, have the spectator hold the deck in hand as though ready to deal. *"Please turn the cards face up onto the table one at a time, calling out the name of each card as you go. Do not change the tone of your voice when you come to your card and do not tell me if we pass it. Go!"*

As he is doing this you are listening for a Five. If the next card called is *not a Three*, it is his selected card. At that moment shout: *"STOP! That is the card you selected. I have it in my mind's eye."*

Do As I Do

In this effect the key card will be the one on the bottom of the deck your spectator is holding. Use two decks of contrasting color.

"Two new decks of cards. Sir, I'd like you to select the one you prefer to use; I'll take the other one." Allow him to pick up one.

"This is an experiment in observation. I want you to watch me very closely. See if you can follow my every move. Do as I do. Ready?"

Shuffle your cards. Allow the spectator to shuffle his in the same manner. *"That's very good. Have you ever done this before?"* Cut your deck in half and replace the cut. Make sure the spectator does the same. Now riffle the edges of the cards with your thumb, merely to make some noise. The spectator should follow this. *"You're very observant."* Turn your deck face up and then face down again in your hand. The spectator will repeat this action. During that time it is important that you see the face-up card on the bottom of his deck. This is your key, so remember it. *"You're terrific! Now put your finger in the center of the deck, take one card out, remember it, and put it on top of the pack."* You do the same thing, but do not pay any attention to the card you draw. His card is now on top of his deck. Ask him to *"Cut the deck in half so we lose the card in the middle."* You do the same. After he has done this, request that you exchange decks. *"Let's swap. You take my deck and I'll take yours. You find your card and I'll find mine. When you have it, put it face down on the table."*

Run through your cards (his pack), looking for the key card you saw earlier. His selected card is directly under (or to the right of) the key. Remove this card and place it on the table, face down.

"You have been doing everything I have done exactly the same way. Isn't it logical that if we both did the same things, we also selected the same cards? Not really, it would be more than a coincidence if that happened, wouldn't it? We won't call it coincidence. I call it magic!"

Turn both cards face up and take your bow.

Three in a Million

You will need two ordinary decks with contrasting back designs. The decks are placed on the table and your spectator is allowed a choice of either one. *"Here is a game of follow the leader. If you do as I do we'll see some unusual results."* Shuffle your pack. He does the same. When you have done this, note the top card of your deck. This is your key card. Remember it. Exchange packs with him. Your key is now his top card. Instruct him to *"Pull a card out of the center, look* *at it, remember it, and place it on top of the deck."* You go through the same motions, but you need not look at the card you pulled out. *"Cut the deck and replace the cut."*

His selected card is now above your key. *"Let's look through our decks to make sure the card is still there."* As you do this you will look for the duplicate of your key. Pull it out and place it on top of your pack. Now look for the matching card in the opposite suit. (Example: Your key is the Two of Clubs. The "opposite card" will be the Two of Spades.)

"I have just done some hanky panky. Let's exchange decks again. Find your card in my deck and place it on the table." You will take his pack and look for your key. The card to its left in the face-up spread is his chosen card. Leave the key card on top and find its duplicate, which you will put on the bottom of the deck as before. Place his card on the table. You should now have two cards on the table, his and yours.

"Please cut a small packet from the top of your deck and hold it for a moment." Point to the table, near the other cards. Try to estimate the size of his cut, and cut as close as possible to the same amount from your pack. *"Let's see if we both have the same amount of cards."* Have him count his cards onto the table, reversing their order. You do the same with your cards. If you hit it correctly, it's an extra plus. If not, add or take away the right amount of cards to make the piles even. The balance of the deck is set aside, next to the other two piles. You now have three groups of cards—a single card, a small packet, and the rest of the deck.

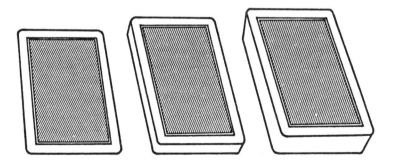

"It would be quite a coincidence if the bottom cards of both decks match, wouldn't it?" Turn the larger pack face up and show the bottom cards to be the same. *"It would be*

even more startling if the bottom cards of the smaller packets match." Show that they do. *"The odds are three in a million that we both selected the same cards."* Now turn up the single cards and show that they also match. *"That's the advantage of being a magician."*

Spelling
Tricks

♠♣♥♦ Using playing cards to spell out words or names. Each card represents a letter.

Your Card Is Here

Two spectators assist with this one. Select one who will be the magician, the other the spectator.

"It takes many years to become a magician. In fact I had to go to a School for Magicians to learn my craft. Here is one of the tricks they taught me, which I will teach you right now. First, we'll need someone to play the part of the magician. How about you?" Point to any person nearby. Select another person to be his victim. Hand the pack to the new magician, but look at the bottom card before you do. This will be your key card. Instruct the magician:

"Spread the cards a bit and let your victim, I mean spectator, take any card. Tell him to remember it." Watch while he does this. *"Now ask him to put the card on top of the deck. Fine. Now cut the deck so that his card is in the middle."* This will bring your key next to the selected card. Take the cards from the "magician." Spread them face up, running through the cards until you find your key. Cut the pack so that your key is on the top. *"Show your spectators that the deck is real and not all of the same card."* Hand the pack to the "magician." Ask him to spread the cards as you did. He is then to close the pack.

"Now deal five cards onto the table, one at ,a time." He does this. *"Pick up the five cards and leave the deck. Now spell the words 'Here is your card.' Duck a card under for each letter you spell. After each word, set the next card on the table."* The first four cards go under his pack, the fifth one on the table. He then spells the other words the same way. When he has spelled all of them, the last card remaining in his hand is the selected card, which he will show to the spectator. Tell him: *"You are now a magician."*

Double Speller

This is another spelling trick, using the key card to locate the selected card, but the unusual example you set makes the trick twice as startling.

Have the spectator select a card, and, using your key card, you locate it in the pack. Cut the deck so that the selected card will appear on top. Now turn the deck so that it is face up.

Let us say for example that the spectator selected the Nine of Clubs. You will push off cards from the face of the pack into the right hand, sliding one under the other. For every card, you will mentally spell out another letter in the name of the selected card. (Nine of Clubs = eleven cards.) The last letter will be the S. Note the very next card. Let us say it is the Ace of Spades. Continue to spell the Ace of Spades. When you have finished, cut the deck at that point and put all the cards in your right hand under those in the left. While you are counting, you will be talking:

"I'm going to spread these cards slowly and I'd like you to look for your card. Don't tell me when you see it; just look to see if it is here." After you have cut the deck, ask the spectator: *"Did you see your card in that group?"* He will, of course, say *"No."*

Turn your pack face down. *"Perhaps we can find your card by spelling it. For example, suppose it's the Ace of Spades.* Name the second card you spelled. *"You will then spell the name by placing a single card on the table for each letter."* You demonstrate this and when you reach the second S of Spades, turn it up to show that you have spelled the correct card. Hand him the deck and allow him to spell his card. *"What was your card? Please spell to it."* He will do so, to everyone's amazement.

What's in a Name?

Everyone likes to make a name for himself. This one makes use of the spectator's name, which will flatter him while you amaze him. Hand the shuffled pack to the spectator as you turn your back.

"Please THINK of any number between one and ten. Now look at the card that is positioned at that number. For example, if your number is nine, look at the ninth card. Leave the card in its original position when you have done this."

Take back the deck after he has indicated that he followed your instructions.

"Let me take the deck behind my back and make a few changes."

When the deck is behind your back, turn it face up. Hold the pack in your left hand and, using your right thumb, pull off the face-up cards one at a time, spelling your spectator's name. Take off one card for each letter in his name. For example, if his name is Bob Jones, you would take off three cards for Bob and five more for Jones. When this has been done, the cards in your right hand are placed under the face-up deck. Turn the deck face down and bring the cards out in front of the audience.

"I have just moved your card away from its original position. What was the number you selected?" (Let us assume he picked number three.) *"Three? One. Two. Three."* Deal off three cards and turn up the last card. *"Is this your card? It isn't . . . because I moved it."* Hand the deck to the spectator. *"We know it's your card because it has your name in its location. Please spell your name, dealing a single card for each letter.* When he reaches the last letter have him name his card. Then turn over the last card he dealt and reveal the card he had selected.

A Spell of Luck

Before you begin you have stacked four Aces on the bottom of your deck. Place the deck on the table and push the cards across in a ribbon from left to right. Ask the spectator to *"Take any card you like from the middle of this spread."*

While he is looking at his card you pull the spread together and pick up the deck. Cut the top half and place it on the table. *"Remember your card, please, and set it on top of the pack."* Drop the remaining cards on top of these, but allow them to dribble down in bunches. Pressure from your index finger will give them a spring action to make the handling look more impressive. *"Your card is now lost in the middle of the pack. Let's see if I can find it."* Turn the deck so the cards are facing you. Look for the Aces. Cut the deck at that point so that all the Aces are now on top. The card immediately following the Aces is the one he selected. *"Hold out your hand please."* Count the five top cards onto his palm one at a time, reversing their order. *"I believe your card is one of these. You're going to help me find it."*

Instruct the spectator to spell the words "THIS IS MY CARD" by shifting one card from the top to the bottom for each letter he spells. After each word, the top card of the deck is placed on the table. (Example: The first word is spelled T-H-I-S. He will place the top card under the pack for the first letter. The next card goes under also, until four cards are transferred. The very next card goes to the table.) When he is through with the spelling he will be left with a single card. *"What was the name of the card you selected?"* He names it. *"Please turn that card over."* It will be a surprise. Now, for a second surprise: *"You had a pretty good poker hand, too."* Turn up the four Aces.

Spelling Test

This one is a fun trick for an intimate group. It can be done on a stage as well, using giant-sized playing cards. You will need nine cards of one suit and a Joker. The cards are arranged as follows, from top to bottom: 3-5-Ace-7-9-2-Joker-8-6-4.

"This is a simple game called 'Spelling Test.' I'd like someone who can spell. How about you, sir?"

Point to someone and ask him to step up to help you.

"Here's what we're going to do. We will spell the names of all the cards. For every letter we will take a card from the top of the pack and place it underneath. The last letter of every word will be the card we spell. Let me show you."

Begin to spell A-C-E. Take the top card and place it on the bottom. Do the same with the second card. Announce the letter "E" and turn up the Ace, placing it on the table. Do the same with the T-W-O. Place the "O" card face up on the table next to the Ace. It will be the Two. Explain once more, spelling the T-H-R-E-E. After removing the Three spot and placing it on the table, hand the deck back to the spectator.

"See how simple it is! Have you got the idea? Please spell Four."

As he is ducking the cards under the deck, one at a time, you spell aloud with him: *"F-O-U-R. Turn up the last card."* He will turn up this card and reveal the Joker. *"I don't think you followed me. I don't need the Joker."* Take the cards back in your own hand. **Put the Joker on top of the stack.** Count again, placing the Joker on the bottom as the first letter, F of "F-O-U-R." Turn up the last card ("R") it will be the Four spot. Hand him the deck again. *"Have you got it now?"* Ask him to spell F-I-V-E. He does this and once again the last card he calls will be the Joker. Place the Joker back on top each time it turns up. Take his cards and you spell *"F-I-V-E,"* which proves to be correct again. Allow him to spell the Six. *"Here's an easy one—only three letters. Now, don't get it wrong."*

He will again spell the Six and reveal the Joker. Take the cards back. *"I'm going to show it to you once again . . . very, very slowly. Look. 'S.' One card goes on the bottom. 'I.' Another one on the bottom."* (Point to the top card.) *"This card is 'X.'"* (Turn it up and set it on the table with the other.) *"It's a Six. Now is that so hard? Watch it again. I'll do Seven. . . ."*

Repeat the spelling with number seven.

"E-I-G-H-T, in case you've forgotten. . . ." Hand him the deck and of course he will spell to the Joker again. At this point you look a bit exasperated. Hand the cards to another spectator. *"Would you like to show him what we mean? Spell EIGHT."* The second spectator will come up with the correct card. Take the cards back and hand them to the first fellow.

"You must see how easy it is. There are only two cards left. Please spell the Nine. N-I-N-E." He will take the cards and spell to the Joker again. Take the cards back. *"Wrong. N-I-N-E"* spell the word putting a card under for each letter and you come up with the Nine. Hand him the Joker. *"Since you seem to favor it so much, I'd like you to take this home and frame it as a reminder that you failed our spelling test."*

In the event that you have no Joker in the deck you may use a Queen, commenting to the spectator: *"I can see that in school you were too busy with the ladies to learn how to spell."* A final reminder: when it comes up, always replace the Joker on top of the pack before spelling again.

Aces

 Since the Ace is the highest card in the deck in most games, it commands the most respect. Tricks done with Aces always receive attention. They are also quite good visually as they can be seen from a good distance away.

European Aces

Frank Garcia used this miracle to astound a group of magicians he met on a recent European lecture tour. The four Aces are used in this effect. They are stacked so that the Aces are located in the seventh, twelfth, and eighteenth positions from the top of the deck. The last Ace is on the bottom. Hold the deck in a dealing position. *"We're going to select a few cards at random."* Turn to your first spectator and ask that he or she give you a number *between* five and ten. Accent the word *"between."* The number the spectator gives you will determine the way in which you count the cards onto the table. If he or she gives you the number *SIX*, you deal the cards onto the table in multiples of *two.* Push two cards off the top and drop them onto the table together. The next two are dropped onto the first two, the last two on top of the whole pile. Place the very next card on the table, off to the side. *"Two-four-six. This card we'll save for later."*

If he calls *SEVEN*, repeat the above. Count by two's and place the seventh card on the table

EIGHT—Count by two's again, placing eight cards on the table in a pile. The top card will be set aside.

NINE—If he calls *"Nine"* you will count by three's. Three cards at a time are pushed off the top. *"Three-six-nine."* The top card is placed aside.

No matter what number has been selected, the card you set aside will be the first Ace. You must now put all the cards from the pile on the table directly on top of the deck. Go to your second spectator. *"Will you please give me a number between ten and fifteen."*

ELEVEN—Fan five cards from the top of the deck and drop them onto the table in a bunch. Count by fives. (*"Five-Ten-Eleven."*) Drop the eleventh card next to the other one set aside on the table.

TWELVE—Deal five, five, and then two. The top card will be the Ace.

THIRTEEN, FOURTEEN—Deal by fives, and then either three or four to get the Ace.

The remainder of the pile will go back on top of the deck. You ask the last spectator for a number *"between fifteen and twenty."* You will deal by fives again, adding one to five cards depending upon the number the spectator selects. Set aside the top card. You will now have three Aces on the table. Put all the cards back on top of the deck. You will now cut the deck in half using the key cut. This means you will pull the bottom half away from the deck with the right hand. Turn the bottom card face up. It will be your last Ace.

BOTTOM HALF

"Let me cut the deck somewhere in the middle."

"I cut the deck at random and found an Ace. You all selected cards at random as well. What have you found?" Turn all three cards over, exposing the Aces. *"Would you call this a coincidence? I wouldn't. I call it a miracle!"*

Your Favorite Ace

Prepare the deck by placing four Kings on top of the deck. Now place the four Aces on top of the Kings. Set the deck in front of the spectator.

"Please cut a small number of cards from the top of the pack and hand them to me." Take the cards and hold them in dealing position. *"I'd like you to deal four piles onto the table."* Demonstrate this by dealing three top cards onto the table. Use the fourth card to scoop up the cards just dealt and place all four on the bottom of your pile. Hand the packet to the spectator. He will deal all the cards into four piles. The top card of every pile he deals will be an Ace. After he has dealt, ask: *"Which is your favorite Ace?"* No matter which one he names, ask him to turn the top card of any packet to reveal an Ace. If he hits the right one, you have an amazed onlooker. Allow him to turn every top card over. *"You have dealt the four Aces. I'm glad you didn't deal from the bottom."* Turn each packet over and you will reveal the Kings on the bottom.

Four-Ace Opener

Sometime before the trick, steal the four Aces from the deck and tuck them under your belt, behind you, at the small of your back. Put the rest of the cards in their case and you are ready for a miracle.

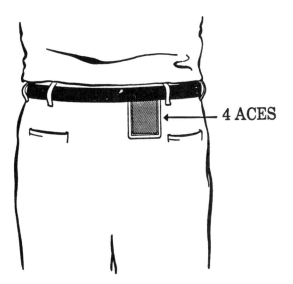

4 ACES

Remove the deck from the case and hand it to a spectator. *"Please shuffle this deck very thoroughly, so that all the cards are mixed."*

Take the cards back and place them behind your back. Pull one of the Aces from under your belt and bring it forward. *"I think I found an Ace."* Show the card and drop it onto the table. Hand the deck to the spectator again. *"Please shuffle them again more thoroughly."* Move the deck behind your back again. This time add all three remaining Aces to the top of the deck. Bring the deck in front of you. *"I have them all now."* Show the three top cards by dealing them face up on the table.

(VARIATION): You can also have the four Aces in your pants pocket facing your body. After the deck has been shuffled, place the deck in the pocket so the Aces are on the bottom. Now announce: *"Let's see if I can find an Ace."* Pull the bottom card out and show it. Do the same with the other three all at once, rather rapidly. You will get credit for having great skill.

Show-Off Aces

Not only do the Aces show off in this trick, but so does the magician. This looks like pure skill, when in fact it is really quite easy.

Have four Aces together in a block near the top of the deck. Spread the cards across the table and allow four cards to be chosen *"from the center of the deck."* Square the deck and give it a cut, so that your Aces will now be somewhere in the center.

"Please remember your cards and hand them to me one at a time as I ask for them." Fan the deck with the faces toward yourself. *"May I have the first card, please?"* Place it in the deck to the left of your first Ace. Allow it to protrude above the other cards by about half a length. *"May I have the second card, please?"* Place this card between the first and second Aces. It will appear to the audience that the cards are going in alongside one another. *"The third card, please."* This one is placed between the *third and fourth* Aces. *"And the last card."* This is placed to the right of the last Ace.

Square the pack and hold the cards in the left hand. The
index finger of the right hand pushes the cards flush with the
pack. This will force four Aces out of the bottom.

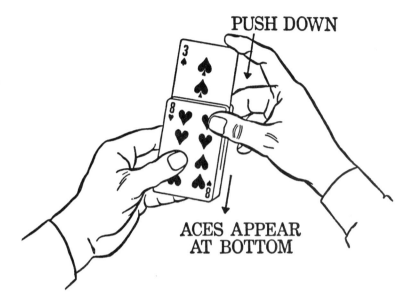

PUSH DOWN

ACES APPEAR
AT BOTTOM

Turn the pack around and spread the four cards as in the
illustration below.

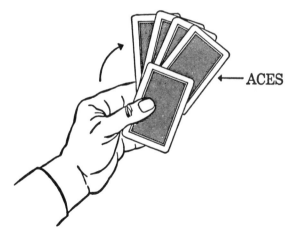

←— ACES

It will seem that the four cards were pushed through the
deck. *"What were the names of the four cards, please?"* After
they name them, you add: *"Those are terrible cards for a
poker game. How about these?"* Turn the pack face up, showing a fan of Aces.

Let's Find Aces

Here is an example of how to vary your magic, using the principles you've used for other tricks.

Before your trick, prepare the deck so that the Aces are the tenth, eleventh, twelfth, and thirteenth cards from the top of the deck. A Nine spot should be the ninth card down. You are now ready to perform.

"Magicians and card players use Aces all the time. Let's find a few Aces. I could go through the deck and look for them, but that's not magic and it's not half as much fun as playing with numbers. May I have a number between ten and twenty?" Count down to the number called, dealing one card at a time. (Example: The number is seventeen.) *"Seventeen. That number has two digits. A one and a seven—that's eight."* (Always add the two digits.) Pick up the cards you dealt and deal them down again. Count them aloud as you deal. At the word *"eight"* turn the card face up. It will be an Ace. Set it aside on the table. The cards remaining in your hand are now dropped onto the pile you just dealt. These cards are all picked up and placed on top of the rest of the deck. *"That's one Ace. Let's find some more the same way. May I have another number between ten and twenty?"* Repeat the dealing as before. Count to the number called. Total those digits. Pick up all the cards and deal to the total. Turn up another Ace. The cards in the hand are dropped onto the cards just dealt. All are picked up and placed on the deck. Do this a third time. *"Another number, please."* Turn up the third ace. *"The last card is the most difficult."* At this time your top card is a Nine spot. Before turning it up, ask for some help. *"Please help me. Everyone say 'ACE, COME UP.'"* Invite them all to say it.

Tap the card a few times and turn it face up. It is a Nine. *"Thanks anyway, folks. I'll work alone. That's a Nine. That means more counting. Nine. . . ."* Deal the cards, counting as you deal. The ninth card is your last Ace.

Cut the Kings

Before the beginning of the trick, secretly stack the deck. Place the four Aces on top of the deck with four Kings directly on top of them. Hand the deck to the spectator. (Kings are the topmost cards.)

"You look like a card dealer. Take the pack and deal down two piles, alternating the cards." Allow him or her to deal out about half the deck. *"You may stop at any time you wish."* Take the rest of the cards from your victim and direct again: *"Now pick up one of those piles and deal that pile into two piles. Do the same with the last packet so that we will have four piles of cards."* At this point you have a King on top of every pile, with an Ace directly beneath it.

"Please turn up the top card of any pile. That's a King. Turn over another one. Isn't that a coincidence—two Kings?" Allow the spectator to turn the last two and he or she has found four Kings. Discard the Kings face up on the table.

"Are you a poker player? What beats four Kings? Four Aces? Right!" Make a magical pass over the cards and turn all the top cards face up to reveal the Aces.

Women's Lib

Try to vary the kinds of tricks you do in any evening's entertainment. This one can be done with Aces, but for the sake of variety we will use four Queens. These are placed on top of the deck before you begin your routine.

Hand the deck to your helper. *"Please cut the deck into four equal piles."* As he does this, keep an eye on the pile that contains the top four Queens. This one must be the last pile on either end of the group.

FOUR QUEENS ON TOP

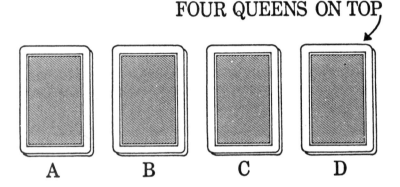

A   B   C   D

"Let us give each pile a name. How about Fred, Mary, John, Pete? No, that's too hard to remember. How about A, B, C, D?" Point to each pile as you name them in order. Make sure pile D is the last one you name.

"Pick up Pile A and deal three cards onto the table where the pile was. Now deal the next three cards, one at a time on top of each of the other piles, in any order you wish." When this has been done, instruct him to put the pile back on top of the three cards he dealt. Repeat the instructions for piles B, C, and D. Each time make sure the first three cards are dealt down before the next three are circulated. When he is through you will have a Queen on top of each pile. *"Now that you've mixed the cards quite thoroughly I'll tell you a secret. This is called the Women's Lib trick. The reason is simple. In this trick, the women always come out on top."* Turn up the Queens.

Aces Follow Aces

Once you have found four Aces (or Kings, etc.) by one of your ingenious methods, you'll need something to do with them. This one is a natural follow-up to combine two tricks to form a routine.

Deal the four Aces face up across the table. Deal three more cards directly below each Ace on the table so you have four rows of three cards with an Ace in front of each row.

"I'm going to place one Ace on the bottom of each pile." Do this by turning the Ace face down and slipping it under the pile. Place the rest of the deck aside. Pick up each pile from left to right, placing one on top of the other. *"The cards are now arranged so that every fourth card is an Ace."* Deal out four cards. Lift the fifth card off the top and use it to point to the last card you dealt. *"The Aces will end up in this pile."* Place the card that is now in your hand *under* the packet you are holding. Turn the fourth card up, showing that it is actually an Ace. Turn it face down again and deal out all the cards from left to right. You will now have only one Ace at the bottom of the fourth pile, and three Aces on top of the third. *"Aces follow Aces. Where one Ace goes, the others follow."* Slip out the bottom Ace of the fourth pile. Show it. Remove the bottom card of the third pile and place it under the fourth pile. Put the Ace in its place beneath the third pile. Tap piles one, two, three, and four with your finger. *"Aces follow Aces."* Turn up pile three to show four Aces.

Poker
Tricks

♠♣♥♦ Card players appreciate these tricks more than others. People are always interested in gambling games where the element of chance is involved. Many early card ruses developed from crooked gamblers of the seventeenth and eighteenth centuries are still in use today.

Never Play with Strangers

Inevitably, after doing a few card tricks, someone will say: *"I wouldn't play cards with you!"* or *"Say, do you know how to cheat at poker?"* The answer is one more trick, but this time under the guise of explaining how card cheats operate.

"Let me show you the principle involved in cheating at poker. First of all, the gambler or cheater needs a good hand. Let me pick out a good one." Look through the cards, pulling out a red King and four Aces. But while you are looking for these cards, find the Ten, Jack, Queen and King of Spades which you will place on the top of the deck. You can do all this rather openly since no one sees the cards, which are facing you. Once you have found the Spades, you can then find the last Ace and drop it to the table. Arrange the cards on the table so the four Aces are together, with the King on top. The Ace of Spades should be on the bottom of the spread.

"This seems to be a good hand for the cheater. Four Aces and a King." Pick up the cards and place them on the very bottom of the deck, with the Ace of Spades showing. *"The cheater will find a nice hand and will place these cards on the bottom, ready for some bottom dealing. This means exactly*

Let me show you." Begin to deal five hands of poker onto the table.

"*We'll assume five people are playing. The first four people will get the cards from the top as they fall. The dealer takes his from the bottom."* Deal the first four cards and then obviously go to the bottom for the fifth card. Repeat this until all five hands have been dealt. Make sure that each time you take one from the bottom you make it quite obvious in a neat fashion. Once the cards are on the table you continue your patter. "*So you see the cheater has the advantage by dealing from the bottom. Naturally, when he does this he must do it more quickly than I have been doing it. Then again, if I could do it quicker I might not be here showing it to you."* Begin to pick up each hand from left to right and place the cards on top of the deck. Your cards go on top, last. "*But dealing from the bottom is often too risky. I prefer to use another method that is known as the stack method."*

As you say this, cut one third of the cards from the top and place them on the table to your left. Cut the next third in front of you. Put the remaining cards to your right. Now your right hand picks up the first pack (Diagram 1), places them on the middle pack (Diagram 2) and places the whole works on the right pack (Diagram 3). (This is known as a "false cut." The cards apparently were cut but they have not changed position.)

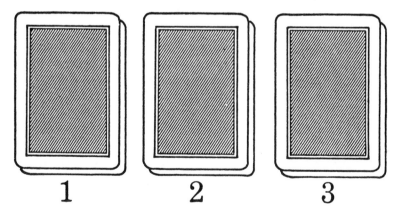

1   **2**   **3**

"*I prefer to deal from the top and still keep the good hand for myself."* Deal five hands again. This time all the cards will come from the top of the deck. When you are ready to deal your own card (the fifth), pretend to make a quick movement or cover the cards for a moment to give the spectators the idea that you may really be dealing a quick one from the bottom. After all the cards have been dealt, continue your patter: *"Just for the sake of curiosity let's see what the other players have. I have the four Aces and have them all beaten."* Turn up the first hand, show it quickly, and turn it face down again. Do the same with the second hand. The third hand is dropped face up on the table. The spectators will see an Ace. Pretend not to notice as you turn up the fourth hand. *"I have Four Aces and have all these people beaten."* At this point someone is sure to tell you about the Aces they saw. *"Oh, my! Sometimes accidents do happen. There is only one way to correct a dealing mistake like that. That is with a hand like this!"* Turn your hand up to expose the Royal Flush. *"Now that you know something about poker, would you care to play a small game?"* The answer is most assuredly going to be *"NO!"*

Jacks or Better

Gambling tricks are always popular, since people are always interested in the ways people win. This one shows how cheaters work.

The deck is stacked as follows, from the top card down. A red Jack, a black Jack, another red Jack, an Ace, a black Jack, another Ace, any card, an Ace, any card, and the last Ace. These are placed on top of the deck.

"Card cheats are known to deal from the bottom and from the middle of the deck. There is also something known as the "second deal." This is when the dealer will deal the second card rather than the top card, so that he can keep a good top card for himself. I'll give you a simple demonstration by using three Jacks, which I prepared by placing them on top of the deck."

Show the three top cards and put them back in the same order. *"I'm going to deal out a few cards and you will still have all three Jacks in your hand. Watch!"*

Deal the cards as follows: The top card to the spectator, the next card to yourself. The third goes to the spectator, the fourth to yourself, and the fifth to the spectator. Now deal off the sixth card, but slide it **under** the two you have in front of you. Pick up your hand and drop it on the top of the deck.

Turn his cards face up on the table. He has two red Jacks on top of a black Jack. Slide the top red Jack under the other two and turn all three cards over, putting them back on top of the deck. *"I'll do it again and maybe you can catch me."* Repeat the deal exactly as before. Make sure you slide your third card under the other two. He will now again have three Jacks. (This time the black Jack will be a different one, but it will go unnoticed.) Show the three Jacks, face up. *"Three Jacks again. Did you catch it that time?"* Turn the Jacks face down, sliding the top one under the other two before putting them back on top of the deck. *"I'll do it one more time."*

Repeat the action again, exactly as before. Show him the three Jacks, but this time you can just drop them on top of the pack as they are.

"Let's deal a hand to see how it comes out." Deal a two-handed poker game from the top of the deck. (Five cards to each player.) Show him that he has three Jacks. Then turn your hand up. *"Jacks are better than nothing, but Aces are better than Jacks."*

I Win, You Lose

This little routine was once used by card sharks to fleece innocents out of their ready cash. We play it as a "fun" game. It is so simple it must be successful.

Openly take out three Tens, three Kings and three Aces. As you do this, secretly get a Nine spot to the top of the deck. Hand the spectator the cards you removed. *"We're going to play a little game called 'I win, you lose.' Shuffle the cards thoroughly."* Take his cards and place them on top of the deck, then hand him the pack.

"Please deal two poker hands. It's just you and me." When he finishes the deal you will announce: *"Good! I win, you lose. Turn your cards over."* Both of you will turn your hands over and, of course, you will win. The principle is simple. Whoever gets the odd card (the Nine) will lose. *"Let's play this again. I'll deal."* Scoop up all the cards, making sure the odd card is on top. If you use it to scoop up the others it will get to the top naturally.

"This time we'll play draw poker." Spread the cards across the table face down. (We are only using the ten cards from the last hand.) *"Who shall draw first?"* It makes no difference who draws as long as you keep an eye on the top card, which is the Nine. It is on top of the spread. Each of you will draw one card from the batch. In the event that you are left with the Nine, you must add a new rule. *"Let's gamble. You give me one of your cards and I'll give you one of mine."* You will, of course, give him your Nine. You must remember its position on the table. *"I win, you lose."* Each of you turns your hands up and you win again.

"You seem to be having a rather poor run of luck. Let's try one more game. Perhaps we can play stud poker."

Get your odd card to the top of the pack again. Deal the Nine face down to the spectator, deal one card for yourself, face down. Turn the other cards face up in an open spread. *"Look, suppose you change your luck. Pick out the four cards you'd like to have."* Let him take any four cards, after which you take the balance and you announce: *"I win, you lose."* Turn up both hands. *"Care to play again for money?"*

Poker Mental

Mind-reading tricks are always fascinating. Couple a mental stunt with a poker trick and you have a winner. Borrow a deck and have it thoroughly shuffled. Now deal out a five-handed game of poker, one hand to each of four spectators, the last hand to yourself. Each player gets five cards.

"I would like each of you to think of one of the cards in your hand. Do not tell anyone else the name of the card. Please remember it." Instruct them to shuffle their poker hands after they have thought of a card. You shuffle your poker hand as well. Gather all the hands face down, beginning with the first spectator on your left. Place his cards on top of the deck. Collect the cards from left to right, the second hand going on top of the first one and so on. Your cards are added to the top, last. At this point you have the deck stacked for the trick. If you care to make the effect more interesting you may use the false cut described in the "Never Play with Strangers" trick.

"We have each selected a single card mentally. Let me deal another round of poker." Deal five hands again, face down. Pick up the first hand to your left. *"Does anyone see his card here?"* Fan the cards so they can all be seen, face up. If anyone sees his card it will be in the exact position from the left of the fan as the position of the spectator himself. That is: If spectator number two sees his card, it will be the second card from the top of the fan. You will now bring the fan under the table and pull out the correct card, tossing it to the table face down in front of the spectator. You can do the same with each hand. Sometimes no one will see his card. Go to the next set. Many times several people will see their cards in the same spread. You still find the cards in the same manner, setting each card in front of its owner. When all the cards have been set out you ask them to name their cards and turn them face up one at a time to verify the miracle.

To make the trick more spectacular you can have yourself blindfolded after dealing the second group. You can still find the selected cards by counting them with your fingers from left to right. The blindfold will make the entertainment more dramatic.

Poker Dream

This is a poker trick that requires a simple set-up and will usually get both laughs and applause.

The cards are set up from the top down, as follows:

King of Spades—(Face down on top of the deck)
Any Ace—(Face up)
Any King—(Face down)
Jack of Spades—(Face down)
Ace of Spades—(Face down)
Any Ace—(Face up)
Any King—(Face down)
Queen of Spades—(Face down)
Any Card—(Face down)
Last Ace—(Face up)
Ten of Spades—(Face down)

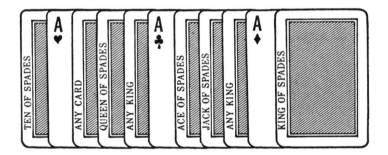

With these eleven cards secretly on top of your deck you're ready to tell a most unusual story.

"Let me tell you about a crazy dream I had last night. You know how dreams are sometimes so real and yet so weird and abstract. I was invited to play poker with a Mississippi hustler. Nothing unusual. He looked just like you or me, except that he had a big green mustache, a wide brimmed hat and a thin cigar sticking out of his mouth. When he smiled, his teeth would sparkle and shine in gold and silver. He looked a lot like a girl I once used to go with, except for the green mustache. Anyway, we started to play the game. As I began to shuffle the deck he said, 'Hold it. In this game we shuffle Mississippi style.' And he proceeded to shuffle this way. . . ."

The deck is on the table in front of you. Cut the top half to the left.

Turn the right-hand packet upside down and shuffle these cards into the left half. Make sure that the top eleven cards remain on top on the left-hand packet. Turn the deck upside down twice. The stack is still on top and the spectator is amused and confused. Continue your story:

"The hustler began to deal. One for me and one for him. And this is how it turned out."

Deal the hands, giving yourself a card and then dealing a card for the gambler opposite you. The dealer will draw three face-up Aces.

"He drew three Aces and won the game."

Pick up the gambler's hand and place the cards, as they are, on top of the deck. Now pick up your cards and put them on top of the rest, without showing them.

"That was a crazy dream. The gambler said it was my turn to deal. So I shuffled the pack . . . Mississippi style."

Repeat the original shuffling process. Cut the top half off and turn the other half upside down. Shuffle the bottom cards into the bottom half of the deck without disturbing the top eleven cards. If you want to make it more confusing, pull some cards from the middle, turn them upside down and put them on the bottom. This will still not disturb the top cards.

"Just as I was about to deal, the hustler winked, and a spark flew out of his eye and landed on the top card. I knew he had done something to stack my cards. When he turned to light his cigar I slipped the top card to the middle." (Do this as you talk.) *"In case he stacked the deck, I would ruin it. Then I dealt. . . ."*

Proceed to deal two poker hands, giving the gambler the first card.

This time the gambler again gets three face-up Aces.

"I said to him, 'You're lucky, sir—three Aces.' He said 'No—a full house.'" (Turn his other two cards face up to disclose a full house.) *"Well, I thought he had me beat, but luckily it was only a dream . . . and it was my dream. So I beat him. . . ."*

Turn your cards over to reveal a Royal Flush in Spades.

Winning Aces

If you need something impressive for the card club, this is a winner. You must stack the top of the deck as follows:

X–Ace–XX–Ace–XXX–Ace–XXXX–Ace

The X may represent any indifferent card, two XXs equal two cards, etc. The first indifferent card is on top of the deck. You are now set up to deal a pair of Aces (back to back) in a poker game.

"How many poker hands shall I deal?" If you can false cut the deck, do so. You can deal anywhere from two to seven hands. If your opponent calls "Two" you must get rid of the top card and then deal two poker hands. The dealer gets the Aces. If he calls "Three," get rid of the two top cards before dealing. Follow the formula below for hands four through seven:

Four–Get rid of one top card.
Five–Remove four top cards.
Six–Remove four top cards.
Seven–Add five cards from the bottom to the top.

To add or get rid of cards, merely do so by toying with the deck, then false cutting once more before starting your deal. You will get a good deal of credit for this one.

Shoot-Out Poker

For a whimsical opening trick at the card table, we recommend this one. You will need a rubber band (about 2½ inches) that will be wrapped lengthwise around a block of about twenty cards. Remove the Royal Flush hand from the deck before you prepare this. (Ten through Ace of Spades.) Place the rubber band around the block. Then square the five Royal Flush cards and force them into the center of the block. Hold the block firmly. Add the rest of the deck to the top and place all the cards into the card case, making sure you close the flap. If you relax pressure on the cards, the five cards will move upward, so be very careful.

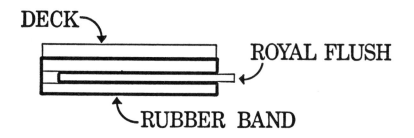

Here's how to present this amusing routine. *"I just got back from Las Vegas where I saw the phantom dealer at work. He's terrific. What's that? You never heard of the phantom dealer? He is the guy who had a patch over one eye and the fastest thumb in the casino. Why, he could deal a winning poker hand to any player he chose. Let me show you how he works."*

Very carefully remove the deck from the case, making sure the five cards do not move out ahead of time. Hold the deck firmly, ready to deal. *"You tell me how many poker hands to deal and which hand shall win."* (Let us say they select five hands of poker with the second hand being dealt the winning cards. Here's how you proceed.) Deal the first card from the top. Pretend to deal the second card but do not put anything down in that position. Actually deal the third, fourth, and fifth hands. Continue to deal the same way again, each time leaving a blank space at the second position but pretending to put a card there. This will bring some laughter. Keep a poker face as you deal, being very serious. *"There they are. Let's see who wins."* Pick up the first hand and show it. Show the third, fourth, and fifth hands. *"Not too good, number two has the winning cards."* The group will be somewhat perplexed. *"If you held the winning hands what cards would you like to have?"* If someone names the Royal Flush you are ready. If no one does, you say, *"I think a Royal Flush is better."* Turn your wrist downward and point the deck at the number two spot on the table. Release the pressure as you move the cards forward. The five cards will shoot out of the deck and land in the right place. Have the spectators look at the hand.

With some practice you can aim the cards to land at any spot on the table. If your friends are actually seated at a card table, deal to each and have him look at his cards. Simply deal in pantomime to number two. *"You can just call me the phantom dealer from now on."* Wait for your belly laughs.

The Force

♠♣♥♦ This is one of the most closely guarded secrets of the magician. We hope that you will consider it sacred. The average person has no idea that he or she can be made to choose a card at the magician's will. It can be a most powerful tool. Use it with discretion.

The Force

It is most helpful in doing card tricks to know in advance which card your spectator will select. You can actually control it so that he picks the card you want him to. This is called a "force"; you are forcing him to pick the one you want him to have.

The card you want to force will be placed on top of the deck. Place the deck on the table in front of the spectator. *"Please cut the cards in half."* Point to a spot on the table and he'll place his half in that position. By pointing in this way you also make sure he does not complete the cut. You pick up the bottom half and place it on top of his half in a criss-cross position.

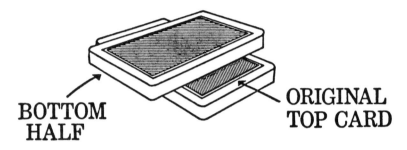

BOTTOM HALF

ORIGINAL TOP CARD

Pause for a moment before speaking. *"Thank you. Do you remember the card you cut?"* Since he hadn't been instructed to see any cards he will, of course, tell you so. *"I'm sorry. Look at that card."* With this statement you proceed to lift the crossed top portion and with your other hand point to the top card of the lower half. This is the original top card and you know what it is. Have him put the card back and you square the deck by replacing your half on top of it and handing him the deck. *"Please shuffle the cards so that I cannot find your card."* You can now reveal the card in any manner you like. To make a mind-reading trick out of this we suggest you have the name of the card written on a piece of paper and placed in an envelope in your wallet. Before announcing the name of the card, remove the envelope and ask him to write his name on it. *"So we know it's the same one."* He then reveals his card and opens the envelope.

Comic Prediction

If you do this one for a large audience use a blackboard so that everyone can see it. When working close-up, use a soft pencil and write the following on a small pad:

THE NAME

OF

THE CARD IS

Have the pad on your table face down. Make sure your pencil has a good eraser.

You will have to force the Ten of Hearts. Use the cut force just described. Have the Ten on top of the deck. After the spectator cuts the deck he will look at his card.

"Just before this performance I made a prediction that I would like someone to read, please." Hand the pad to another spectator to read. He reads: *"The name of the card is. . . ."*

You ask him to *"go on. Read the rest."* He will tell you that there is no more. *"Oh, I am sorry. I was in such a hurry I forgot to finish it."* Pick up the eraser and erase the "H" in the first word, the "AME" in the second. Go to the last line and erase the "T" in the first word, the "C" and "D" in the second. Cross the top of the "I" in the last word, so it looks like a T.

The pad will look like this.

T E N

OF

HE AR TS

"What was your card?" When he names it, turn your pad around so all can see it. If you use a blackboard, turn it around so they cannot see what you are erasing.

Comic Touch

Magic should always be entertaining. Your audiences should be amazed, but they should also have fun. Here is a quick piece of comedy that will be remembered long after many of the astounding ones have been forgotten. You'll need a Nine of Diamonds from an old deck.

Tear the card almost in half, tearing around the pips so that only five diamonds are shown on the face of the card.

This card is placed in your breast pocket, with the torn side down. The card should be facing the audience when it comes out of the pocket. Use the cut force and force the Five of Diamonds. Have the spectator replace the card in the pack and shuffle.

"This is my most famous trick. I haven't missed in sixteen years. Which is unusual by itself since I learned it only three weeks ago. You have a freely selected card, sir, and I have its duplicate in my pocket." Lift the half card up out of the pocket, but only enough to show the first two rows of diamonds and the nine pip. *"And here it is."* The spectators will announce that you are wrong. *"Wrong? Never! What was the name of your card? Five of Diamonds? That's what I have."* Let them correct you a second time. *"If you don't believe me, count them yourself."* Take the half card out of your pocket and drop it onto the table. Don't start talking again until the laughs have subsided.

L'Chaim

Numbers are quite interesting. The title of this trick comes from the Yiddish word that means "To Life." It is often used as a toast. The word is spelled with two Hebrew letters, "Chai," which is the eighth letter of the Hebrew alphabet, and "Yod," which is the tenth letter. The two added together give you the number eighteen, which is considered a lucky number by many Jewish people. The number eighteen is also a very lucky number for magicians.

To prepare this effect you write a prediction that names the card you will force the spectator to choose. You can also make this more impressive if you use a duplicate card from another deck. Seal it in an envelope which is in full view of your audience while you are doing the rest of your magic. Let's say this is the Nine of Diamonds. You will now make sure that the Nine of Diamonds is the eighteenth card down from the top of the deck. You will also need a small pad and a pencil.

"Before we use the cards I'd like someone to please come up here and take this pad and pencil. Thank you. Will you please write down any three digits, making sure the highest value of all three is written first. Thank you. Please reverse the order of these digits and write them below the first three. Draw a line. Now subtract the smaller bottom number from the top one. You have a new number. Add the single digits of this number together. You have now arrived at a smaller number. Will some other party please help us? Pick up the deck and deal one card at a time from the top, counting them until you reach the figure this gentleman has arrived at. By the way, what was that number?" He must answer "Eighteen." The rest of this drama is up to you. You now reveal the card at the selected number to be the same as your earlier prediction.

Selected digits	7 4 2
Reversed	2 4 7
Subtract	4 9 5

Total digits $4 + 9 + 5 = 18$

It is interesting to note that the total will always be eighteen.

The middle digit will always be nine, with the two outer digits totalling nine.

Keeping this in mind, your trick can be more interesting if

you have one card at the eighteenth position and its duplicate in another deck at the ninth position. The first spectator will count to eighteen and turn the card face up. The second spectator will total the digits of 18 $(1 + 8)$ and will look at his ninth card. They will match.

Miracle Prediction

Here's how a force will work in the spectator's hands. The card you want him to pick is on the top of the deck. The same card in another deck is reversed and that deck has been replaced in its case. Both decks are on the table in their cases and you're ready to perform a miracle. *"Here are two decks of cards. Please take one deck—either one."* If he picks up the deck with the reversed card, have him place it in his pocket. *"So no one can touch it."* If he takes the other deck, push the first one aside. *"Remove the pack you are holding from its case and set it on the table."* When he has done this, request that he *"choose any number between one and fifty-two. We're going to deal that many cards, so don't make it too high or I'll have to work overtime."* He will name the number he has chosen. (Example: Eighteen.) You pick up the deck and start dealing one card at a time, counting aloud until you reach eighteen. Then stop and put all the cards you just dealt back on top of the deck. *"Just a moment. If I handle the cards you might think I am doing some of my famous sleight-of-hand. Will you please deal one card for each number?"* Hand him the deck. *"What was that number again? Eighteen?"* He deals to the eighteenth card and you have him place it face down on the table away from the pack. *"By the way, remember the pack in your pocket* [or the one on the table]? *Please open the box and remove that deck. No one has touched it, is that right? Spread the cards face down and you will see something very interesting. One card is upside down. It is the* [name the card]. *Will you please turn up the card you selected. It is the* [name the same card] *again."*

Reds
and
Blacks

♠♣♥♦ The selections here represent the best Red-Black tricks in magic. Each one is an impossible effect. Treat them with respect.

Magnetique

Designed to call attention to your masterful control over cards, this one is almost impossible to beat. The working is really quite simple and all you have to do is riffle shuffle.*

Before the demonstration have all the red cards on top of the deck and all the blacks on the bottom. Begin the trick by handing the cards to the spectator. *"Please deal out four hands of bridge."* He will have four piles when he has finished. *"Please point to any two of those piles, which I will shuffle together."* Do a riffle shuffle, shuffling both packs into one. Now shuffle the two remaining piles together the same way. You have two packs left. Shuffle these together in the same manner.

"Would you say we have mixed the cards rather thoroughly so far?" Cut off about three-quarters of the deck, placing it to the right. Now cut this section, but take off only about a third, setting it to the right again. You will now have three packets. Look through the cards in the center pile and remove a red and a black card. *"These cards will act as magnets."* Show them. *"Let me rub them both on each of these two (outer) packs. There! A miracle! The magnetism of the red card has pulled the reds together; the black card did the same for the blacks."* Turn the two outer packets face up. Each pile contains cards that are all black or all red.

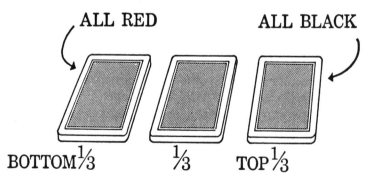

ALL RED   ALL BLACK

BOTTOM⅓   ⅓   TOP⅓

* See Card Handling, which begins page 159.

Under the Table

You might preface this one by explaining that many magicians have sensitive fingers and can find cards by their sense of touch.

Remove six red cards and six black cards, making a single pack of the twelve cards. Secretly arrange them so that they are alternating in color—red, black, red, black, etc.

"Here is a bunch of cards that I would like you to mix in a very special way." Cut the packet a few times as you talk. This will not disturb your arrangement. Hand the packet to the spectator under the table.

"Take these under the table so that no one can see what you're doing. Here is the way you will mix the cards. First, cut the deck in half by putting the top half under the other one. Now, take the two top cards and turn them face up. Cut the pack in half again. Once more, take the two top cards off the deck, and turn them upside down. Cut again. Do this as many times as you like." When he has indicated that he is finished, take the deck back still under the table. Here's what you do under the table—we will call it the "flopover." The pack is in your left hand. Take the top card into your right hand. Now turn the next card upside down and put it on top of the one in your right hand. The next card is dealt as it is. The next one is "flopped" or turned over. Repeat this procedure until all the cards are in your right hand. *"I have just touched all the cards. There are six cards face up."* Bring the deck onto the table. Deal the cards into two piles—face up at your right and face down at your left. Spread the face-up cards to show the six. *"Not only did I predict the number, but I also separated the red ones from the black ones."*

Turn up the face-down cards to show them. Put the two packs together and hand them to the spectator. *"Shuffle these again, please, and hand them to me under the table."* When you get the cards do the flopover again. (This will alternate the cards, face up and face down.) Hand the pack back to the spectator over the top of the table. *"Take these under the table again. Remember how you mixed them before. Turn two over and cut. Do the same a few times more. Are you ready?"* When he is satisfied that he has cut them enough you will continue. *"Now bring the cards into your lap so that only you can see them. If the top card is face down, turn it face up and look at it. Remember it and cut the deck. If the top card is face up, remember it and turn it face down before you cut the deck. You may cut the cards again a few times before you give them back to me."*

He will hand them back to you under the table. As you get them you do your flopover move again. Bring the deck to the top of the table. *"Some are face up and some are face down. Your card may be either. What was the name of that card?"* As soon as he names it, spread the cards across the table. They will all be face down except for his card, which is reversed in the spread.

Color Separation

Almost impossible to figure out, this astounding miracle will amaze even the magicians who see it.

Prepare the deck by separating the red-face cards from the blacks. Set them up in an alternating arrangement. (Red, black, red, black, etc.) Place the deck back in its case and you are ready to begin.

Remove the case from your pocket. Take the cards out and place them face down on the table. *"You are about to see an impossible demonstration of dexterity, mystery, and talent."* As you talk, cut the deck a few times, replacing the cut each time. Hand the deck to someone who knows how to riffle shuffle. If you're not sure he can shuffle this way, do it yourself. Give the deck a good riffle shuffle. Turn the pack face up on the table and ribbon-spread the cards for a moment. *"The deck is completely mixed."* Look at the spread of cards and find any two reds or two black cards that have come together. (There will usually be five or six pairs like this.) In picking up the spread, separate the pair. You can do this by picking up the bottom section first and then the remaining cards, placing them face up on top of the first portion. Turn the deck face down.

"We will need two groups of cards." Start to deal the deck into two heaps, one card to your left, the next to the right, alternating until the cards have been dealt. You will have exactly twenty-six cards in each pile when you finish.

"Will you please pick up either of these piles and hold them in your hand ready to deal?" You pick up the other pile. *"I'm going to ask you to deal the cards face up one at a time, separating the reds from the blacks. If the card is black, place it to your left. If it is red, place it to your right. As you deal each card I will also deal one face down diagonally opposite to your pile."*

For every black card he deals to his left (X) you deal a face-down card diagonally opposite (to your left, B). If he deals a red card to his right (Y) you deal a face-down card to your right (A).

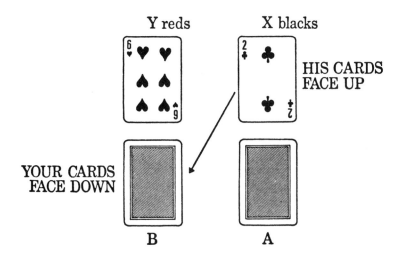

"I shall attempt to match you card for card by color."

Both of you now deal as described above. At the completion of the deal you each have two piles in front of you. *"Something unbelievable has happened."* Turn each of his face-up piles over and place them on top of the face-down piles directly below them. (See the illustration.) Pile X will go on top of pile A, pile Y on top of pile B.

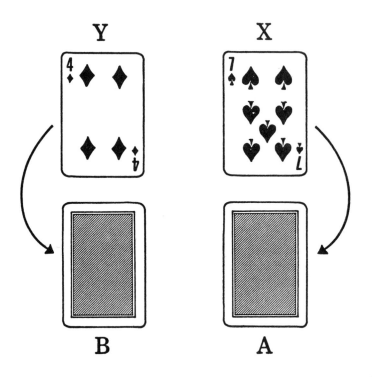

Snap your fingers. *"The snap did it. Watch!"* Turn each pack face up and spread the cards. The reds are in one pile, the blacks in the other.

Intuition

This one can be done as a demonstration of ESP or clairvoyance. It falls into the category of mentalism and should be presented as an experiment rather than a trick.

"It is often said that women have more intuition than men. Intuition is an instinctive feeling that causes you to know something without having to think about it. You just know it. Many people have intuition without realizing it. Let me demonstrate this." While you talk, shuffle the deck. If you like,

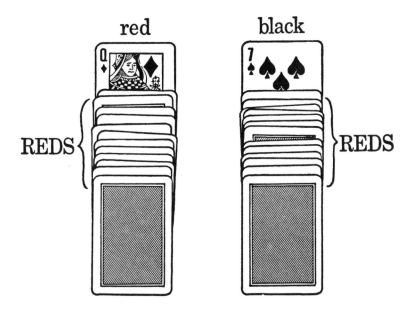

you may have the spectator shuffle the pack. Fan the cards
toward yourself so that you see the face cards. Look at the
top twenty cards and determine whether you have more red
or black cards. You don't have to count them; simply get a
rough idea. Remove a single black card and place it face up on
the table in front of the spectator. Do the same with a red card.

*"We have a red card and a black card on the table. I am
going to remove cards from the deck, one at a time. If you
think the card is black you will call it out and I will place it
on the black pile. If you think it is red I will place it on the red
pile. Got the idea?"*

If you have more reds than blacks in your spread (the top
section) you will begin your trick using reds. If not, you will
use the blacks. (Use whichever you think is predominant in
the spread of twenty cards.)

Let us say you have more reds than blacks. You will now
start removing the red cards one at a time, turning them face
down as you draw them. Place each card on the pile the spectator names. Allow the cards to overlap as you place them in
the piles, so that you can always see the top leader card.
Don't worry about placing the red card on a black pile.

You will continue to pull red cards out of the fan, placing
them on the selected pile until you have about fifteen cards
on the table. *"Let's change the pattern a bit. This time we'll*

put red cards on this side and blacks on the other." Indicate
that you will reverse the position. Pull another red card out
and turn it face up on top of the supposedly black pile. Do the
same with a black card. The cards on the top of your spread
will now be predominantly black. Pull these one at a time and
continue as you did before, placing them where the spectator
will indicate. Do this with about three more cards. Pull a
bunch of black cards away from the pack and turn them face
down on the table. Place the rest of the deck aside. Now take
the black block and shuffle them. Hand this block to the
spectator.

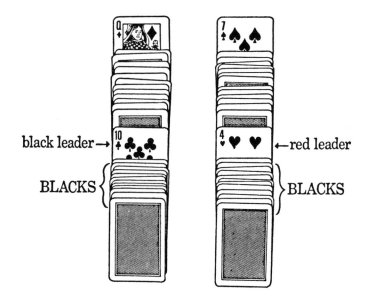

"Would you try this yourself? If you think it's red, put
the next card on the red pile; otherwise deal it onto the black
pile. Do this with one card at a time, so that you have a moment to think."

At the end of this process you have cards on the table as in
the illustration on the next page.

One set of cards will be exactly correct, with red cards following the red leader card and blacks following the black
leader. The other set is just reversed. Push the correct set
toward the spectator. "Will you check to see if you separated
the cards correctly?" As he starts to do this you pick up all the
cards under the top leader (X) and turn them over, spreading
them on the table.

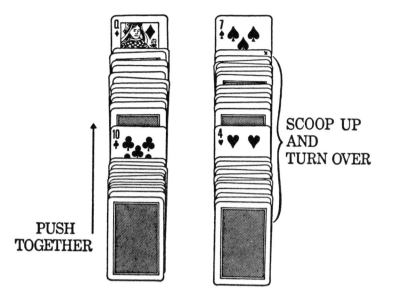

PUSH
TOGETHER

SCOOP UP
AND
TURN OVER

The miracle has been accomplished. *"You have done it!
Call it magic, ESP, or anything you like. I call it intuition."*

Mentalism

♠♣♥♦ Call it mind reading, ESP, or clairvoyance and you have a rapt audience—spectators who want to believe it is real. Do not sell it as the real thing, but, by the same token, don't let on there's a trick to it. Let your audience believe what it will.

An Absolute Miracle

You may present this as a feat of mentalism. If you do this on a stage or platform, build it very dramatically because the result is really impossible. You need two decks. Make sure one of them has been thoroughly shuffled.

The second deck will be set up exactly the same as the first. In other words, the decks will match—card for card from top to bottom. Arrange it so that every **tenth** card is a Ten spot. Put the decks back in their respective cases.

When ready to perform, you will show the two decks. Invite two spectators to come up from the audience. Turn to the first one and say: *"Sir, I'm going to ask you to put one of these decks in your pocket. Either one you select, you will keep. You have a free choice."* He will pick either one. (Each has the same arrangement, so it makes no difference which is selected.) Turn to the second spectator. Pick up the other deck, remove it from its case. Turn it face up. *"Will you select any number between one and fifty-two? Whatever number you choose, this other gentleman will use."* Let us say he picks thirty-three. Turn to the first man. *"Please remember number thirty-three as your number."* Spread the face-up cards in front of the second spectator. You will be looking for your Tens. In this way you can quickly count by tens from the top of the deck to number thirty-three. You must find the card that is thirty-third from the top. Once you see it, cut the pack so that it is now your top card. While spreading the deck you are talking: *"You can see, sir, that this is a regular deck of cards that has not been arranged in any special way."*

You must now force the top card. The best method is the cut force we described elsewhere in the book.* Have the second spectator cut the deck. Place the bottom section across the top for a moment. *"Did you cut freely where you wanted to?"* Lift the top group and point to the top card of the cards on the table. *"Please take that card, but do not look at it. Set it aside."*

Turn to the first spectator. *"Will you remove the deck from the case? The number was thirty-three, am I correct? Please count down to the card that is thirty-three cards from the top of your pack. Do not look at that card; merely set it aside."*

When both operations have been completed you will now

*See p. 64.

begin your acting. *"Gentlemen, I had nothing to do with this experiment except to direct you. One of you selected a number at random. One of you selected a card the same way. It is highly improbable that the two cards you finally selected would be the same. And yet you have both witnessed an absolute miracle."* Point your finger at the cards. *"Turn the cards over."* They are the same.

Mental Selection

This self-working effect is quite mystifying since the spectator never actually picks a card. He will merely think of one.

Begin your experiment with the spectator dealing the deck into four equal piles. *"Please pick up one pile and look at the cards. Think of any one of the cards in the group. Remember the card."*

As he does this you pick up the other three piles and put them together. Add his pile to the bottom of the group. You will now deal six cards, one on top of the other. Do this three more times, giving you four piles. Now deal three cards onto each pile. The next time around you deal two cards onto each pile. Repeat this with the remaining cards. The spectator's card will be among the top four of one of these piles. Fan each pile, allowing him to see the cards. *"Is your card somewhere in this group?"* If he says *"no,"* go on to the next. The pile containing his card is placed on top of the others as you assemble the piles. Begin to deal out four piles. Remark, *"There must be a faster way."* Cut the remaining cards into four equal packs and drop them on top of cards already dealt. Pick up any pile. Note the bottom card and shuffle the pile. Ask him if he sees his card. If he says *"Yes,"* the bottom card you noted was his card. Name it. Should he say *"No,"* keep picking up piles until you come to the right one.

I'll Leave the Room

Husband and wife teams are popular in magic and mentalism. Here's one trick that can be done by both . . . if one of them keeps quiet. You need a confederate for this one.

Lay out nine cards in three rows of three cards each. Hand the deck to your confederate, who will join the group in watching the trick.

"I'll leave the room, and while I am out, will you all please select a single card. You will all concentrate on that card and call me back as soon as you're ready. Oh, yes—please don't forget to call me back!"

When the group has selected a common card, they will call you back. Steal a glance at the confederate's hand. He or she will hold the deck with his or her thumb on the deck at the same relative position as the selected card. You now know the card that has been selected, so the rest is acting. Flounder a bit and finally name the card. Offer to repeat the test, but don't become a ham. After the third time, stop.

Here is how the cards are laid out:

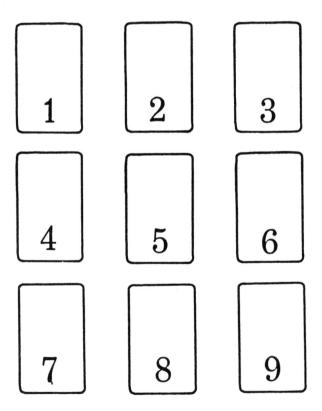

The numbers will correspond to the position of the confederate's thumb on the deck. Therefore if the card at number two has been chosen, the confederate's thumb will be positioned at deck position number two.

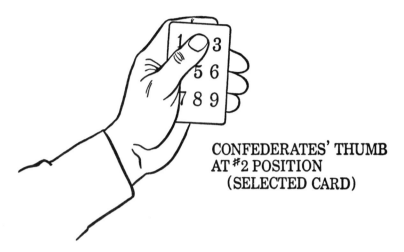

CONFEDERATES' THUMB
AT #2 POSITION
(SELECTED CARD)

Picture-No Picture

After talking about "sightless vision," where blindfolded magicians can apparently see through wads of dough and bandages on their eyes, offer this demonstration.

This is done seated at a table, with people sitting all around you. You may really be blindfolded or you may just close your eyes. Anyone in the audience hands you the deck, which is placed against your forehead so that the faces of the cards can be seen by everyone in your audience. Naturally you cannot see them. Rub your fingers over the first card and announce whether it is a picture or not a picture card. This is done very easily by having a friend or your spouse seated alongside or opposite you. Repeat the action. Each time a picture card comes up your confederate will gently step on your toe.

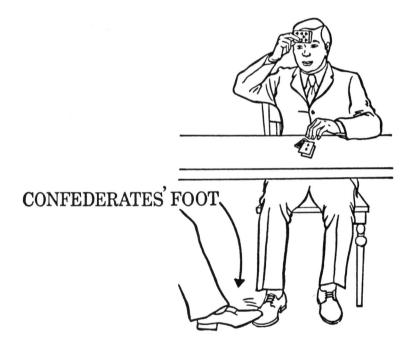

CONFEDERATES' FOOT

Don't pass this one up because it looks simple; the effect is very startling and will dress up your party. It is also a great trick to present over the dinner table at dessert time.

One Out of Five

Acting ability will help a great deal when you are doing mind-reading tricks. The tricks are generally simple, but the presentation makes them astounding.

Prepare this experiment by secretly placing four cards in your pocket, backs out. These should be lying in a horizontal position in the trouser pocket. You are now ready to perform an unusual effect.

Spread the deck face up on the table and allow someone to pick out any five cards. The rest of the pack is not used, but it is left face down on the table. Arrange the cards in numerical sequence so that you can memorize the values easily. Try to remember the five cards by making up a number. (Example: The spectator selected a Three, a King, a Four, a Nine and a Two. You arrange them 2-3-4-9-K and remember the series as 23-49 K.) *"Please think of any one of these cards. Do not tell me what your card is; merely think of it."* Once he has a card in mind, place the five cards in your pocket. These are placed backs out, in a vertical position behind the cards already there.

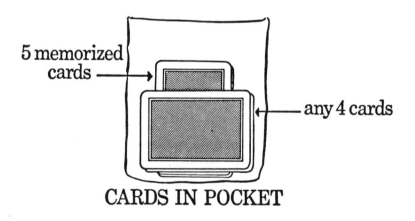

5 memorized cards —→

any 4 cards

CARDS IN POCKET

Pick up the deck casually. *"You are concentrating on your card."* Bring your right hand to your forehead as though deep in thought. *"I think I have it."* Go into your pocket and one by one remove the four horizontal cards that were placed there before. *"I don't think it is any of these. Not this one, nor this, nor this."* After the four cards are removed they go on top of the deck. Your hand goes into your pocket. Slip a finger between each of the cards in the pocket.

"There is now only one card left in my pocket. It should be the one you selected. Which card did you choose, please?" When he names the card you can produce it from your pocket easily. Leave the other cards there and you can repeat the trick.

Simplicity Telephone Test

Over the telephone there is no possible chance that you can manipulate a spectator's cards. This one is an amazing effect, but it is simple to do.

Before calling your victim, get a sheet of paper and list two rows of numbers between one and fourteen. Have your pencil ready and dial your friend.

"If you get a deck of cards I am about to boggle your mind with an experiment in telephonic telepathy." Wait until he gets a deck of cards and then instruct him to: *"Shuffle the cards so they are not in any special order. Now pick out any card, look at it, and place it on the bottom of the deck. Fine. Now cut the deck in half in front of you. Turn both halves face up. Have you done that? One of the cards you are looking at is the card you chose. Take a number of cards from the other pack and transfer them to the top of your card, but add only enough cards to equal the value of your card. For example, if you chose a Deuce you will need two cards; a King is thirteen. Got it? Okay, add those cards to the face of the first pack. Discard the other pile and read off the names of the cards on the face of your pack, one at a time."*

As he begins to read, you disregard his first card but begin to write the names of the cards he calls. The second card he names you will list next to your number one, then list the rest exactly as he calls them. You can abbreviate for speed (Ace of Hearts = AH; Six of Clubs = 6C, etc.).

After he has read fourteen cards (the list is full), stop him. *"Have we passed your card yet? Of course, you have!"* Look at your list and see what card matches the number you wrote. For example, if there is a Nine of Clubs at number nine you have found his card. Should there be two or more cards that match the numbers chosen you will have to "fish." This is how you do it. Let us say there is a Nine of Clubs at number nine and a Jack of Diamonds at number eleven. You might ask, *"I believe your card is a picture card—is that correct?"*

If he says *"Yes,"* you know it's the Jack. If he says *"No,"* you tell him: *"Then it must be a black card . . . a Club . . . a Nine of Clubs."*

Example of your chart.

1.–KH	8.–7C
2.–5H	9.–9C
3.–8D	10.–6D
4.–KD	11.–3S
5.–QH	12.–AH
6.–9D	13.–AS
7.–4D	14.–JH

The Nine of Clubs would be the selected card.

The Mentalist

One of the oldest telephone tricks in magic is still the best. Years ago it was called the Wizard Trick, but with today's terminology we call it the Mentalist. Present this at your next party.

"I have a friend who is probably the best mind reader in the world today. The man is fantastic, he reads thought waves, brain waves, and is an ESP expert. I wish he were here this evening. But wait a minute. I have his phone number and I have an idea. Let's test him to see if he can use his telepathy long distance." At this point in your conversation have a spectator openly select a card from a face-up spread on the table. You have seen this card along with everyone else in the room. Let us say for example that the chosen card was the Four of Diamonds. *"Let's all be quiet, and no one mention the Four of Diamonds. I'll call the Mentalist and you can speak with him. When you get him, ask him to tell you what card we picked. I'll dial, it's an unlisted number."*

Naturally the party you're going to call should know the trick. He can be a close friend or perhaps a member of your family. Dial the number and when he answers you say, *"May I speak to the Mentalist?"* This is the code and he knows that you are doing the trick. He will then begin to name the four suits slowly. As soon as he names the right one (Diamonds in this case) you stop him by saying, *"Hello, Mentalist?"* He will now list the cards quickly, *"Ace, two, three, four. . . ."* You will interrupt as soon as he has named the correct card. *"Hold on for a moment, please."* Hand the phone to the spectator in the room who has chosen the card. He will ask the Mentalist for the name of his card. Have your friend tell him the name but he should do it in stages, such as: *"You have chosen a red-faced card. I believe it is a Diamond. A rather low card. Please concentrate. I think it is the Four of Diamonds. Thank you for calling."* He will hang up immediately. The shock is a good one, but under no circumstances offer to repeat it. And do not disclose the number you dialed.

Quick Prediction

Predicting the future is always fascinating. When someone shows interest in this type of experiment, you can demonstrate with this one. Write your prediction on a sheet of paper. *"You will select the Seven pile."* Fold the paper and place it under an ashtray or a place where no one will try to look at it. Pick up your deck and quickly locate the four Sevens, placing them on top of the deck.

Deal the four Sevens, one atop the other one in a small pile. *"There's one pile."* Deal the next seven cards onto another pile. *"There's another pile. I will ask you to put your hand on either pile. Whichever pile you choose will be the one we will use. Choose carefully."* Pick up the remaining cards and lose them in the deck. *"Will someone now read the prediction?"* No matter which he chose, the prediction will be correct. If he chose the pile of four cards you tell him: *"Turn the cards face up, please."* If he chose the other pile, suggest that he *"Count the cards in that pile, please."* You win either way.

Impromptu Prediction

Someone shoves a deck of cards into your hands and says: *"Do a trick."* Spread the deck facing yourself and remove an Ace, placing it face down on the table.

"There is a prediction of something that is going to happen." Look through the cards again and pull out any two cards and another Ace, placing them face down on the table. Remember where the second Ace is located. Push the first Ace

under a drinking glass or off to the side. *"There are three cards.*
Please pick up any two of them." If your spectator leaves the
Ace, the trick is over. Show the Ace to match your predicted
card. *"I predicted you would choose the Ace."* If he picks up
the Ace along with another card, instruct him to: *"Hand me
either one of those cards."* If he hands you the Ace you will announce: *"You gave me this one out of the three. It matches
my prediction. I predicted you would choose the Ace."* Show
the other Ace. If he hands you the other card and keeps the
Ace for himself you will announce *"You chose that one card out
of three.* (Toss the other one onto the table) *"I predicted you
would choose the Ace."* Turn the other Ace up.

As you can see, the magician cannot lose. This is called the
"Magician's Choice" and will also work with coins or small
objects.

Astounding Prediction

On arrival at a friend's house for a party, hand the hostess an
envelope. Ask her to sign her name on it and to put it in a
prominent place in the living room. The prediction inside will
read: *"This evening 'John Smith' will select the Nine of
Clubs."* You can make it more interesting by predicting the
time, but you must be sure you start your trick five minutes
earlier. Of course you must know one of the people who will
be at the party. You will use him for your spectator.

Now for the trick. Be sure that the predicted card lies
twenty-one cards from the top of the deck. Set the deck on the
table. *"I need help for this one. How about you, John?"* Select
the person whose name you predicted, in this case 'John
Smith.' *"Please cut off about a quarter of the pack and hold
on to those cards until we need them."* Pick up the remainder
of the pack and begin to deal cards onto the table from right to
left. Make sure each card overlaps the one before it. Each card
should be showing. Deal twenty cards and stop. *"John, you
don't know how many cards you have there, do you? Perhaps
we should count them."* Have someone verify the count. Let
us assume he has twelve cards. *"Twelve! Okay, let's count
twelve cards."* Start counting cards from left to right setting
the twelfth card aside. *"John, we came to this card strictly by
chance. We had no idea how many cards you were going to cut*

90   *to.*" Point to the envelope that has been in the room all evening. Stress that fact. *"May we have the famous envelope? I will not touch it. Perhaps our hostess will verify her signature across the flap. No one has opened it since she signed it. Please read the contents."* She will read the prediction made earlier in the evening. You can now take bets on local sporting events since you are capable of knowing the outcome in advance.

The Pre-Arranged Deck

♠♣♥♦ The system used here was named for its orig-
inator, Si Stebbins. Stebbins was a vaudeville performer with forty years of experience behind him.
The principle was his; the tricks were developed
by others.

Si Stebbins Master System

For over forty years a man named Si Stebbins had been mystifying audiences of laymen and magicians with his startling card tricks. The stage magician later divulged his method, which is probably the best of its kind in the magic profession. When properly mastered, this system will earn you the reputation of being a miracle worker.

Si Stebbins used a regular deck of cards that was stacked in a special arrangement. Each card in sequence has the value of *three* more than the preceding card. Therefore, if the top card is an Ace, the next card in the series is a Four, next a Seven and so on. The suits rotate in series as well—Clubs first, followed by a Heart, a Spade, and finally a Diamond. If the first card is the Six of Clubs, the next card would have the value of three more in the next suit, the Nine of Hearts. (Jack bears the value of eleven, Queen twelve and King thirteen. See the chart below.) With the deck set in this arrangement you can cut it as many times as you like without disturbing the sequence, and yet by looking at the bottom card you can tell the name of the top card. (Three more in value of the next suit.) To make it easier to remember the arrangement of the suits, you can memorize the word "Chased." Picture it this way: CHaSeD, so that the key letters stand out: Clubs, Hearts, Spades, Diamonds.

SI STEBBINS SET-UP

K—Clubs	K—H	K—S	K—D
3—Hearts	3—S	3—D	3—C
6—Spades	6—D	6—C	6—H
9—Diamonds	9—C	9—H	9—S
Q—C	Q—H	Q—S	Q—D
2—H	2—S	2—D	2—C
5—S	5—D	5—C	5—H
8—D	8—C	8—H	8—S
J—C	J—H	J—S	J—D
A—H	A—S	A—D	A—C
4—S	4—D	4—C	4—H
7—D	7—C	7—H	7—S
10—C	10—H	10—S	10—D

King of Hearts follows Ten of Clubs, etc.

Using the System

Allow any card to be chosen from the deck. After the card has been removed, merely cut the deck at that point and look at the bottom card. Add three in the next suit and you have the name of the chosen card. Be sure to have the chosen card placed on top so that you don't break the chain for the next trick if you decide to do more than one with the deck.

Instant Counting

Hold the deck perpendicular to the floor. The left hand holds the pack while the index and second fingers of the right hand riffle the top right edge of the cards, moving toward your body. Ask the spectator to call *"Stop"* at any time. Break the

deck at that point and hand him the half with the largest number of cards. What you will be doing in the meantime is some rapid calculating. Note the bottom card of your deck. (Let us say it is a King, for example—numerical value of thirteen.) Note the card at the point where you cut the pack. (Let us assume it is a Five.) Subtract the lower number from the higher number and multiply by four. Here is the formula in this case:

Bottom Card	13
Cut Card	− 5
Difference	8
Multiply by Four	× 4
Total	32

You now announce: *"I estimate that you are holding thirty-two cards."*

Have him count them and you will always be accurate. Should the result be lower in number, it will represent the smaller group of cards.

You will always multiply by four. In the event that the bottom card is the same as the cut card, you know that each card is exactly thirteen cards away from its mate, so you can estimate that it is either twenty-six or thirty-nine cards.

The Card in the Middle

You will notice that by using this system each card in the deck has its mate thirteen cards away. By looking at the bottom card you can determine not only the top card but also the card in center of the deck. It will be exactly the same card as the bottom card in its opposite suit. For example, if the bottom card is the Three of Hearts, the twenty-sixth card will be the Three of Diamonds. It will always be of the same color. Here is how to use this factor in performing your trick.

Cut the deck several times rapidly by bringing the bottom half out and placing it on the top. It is the same motion as the key cut described earlier. By doing it repeatedly you give the illusion of shuffling the deck, when, in fact, you are only cutting it. *"While I am shuffling the cards, please call 'Stop' any time you like."* When the spectator stops you, note the bottom card. (Example: Seven of Clubs.) And announce: *"The twenty-sixth card from the top of this deck will be the Seven of Spades."* Allow the spectator to count down to that position and reveal the card. Should you want to repeat the trick you do the counting yourself, turning each card face up, one on top of the other as you deal them onto the table. In this way you do not change the order by counting.

The Joker Knows

For this presentation you will need a Joker. You can add it anywhere in the deck. Remove the deck from the case. *"Many people don't know why there are Jokers in the deck. The Joker represents the court jester, but many kings had their jesters beheaded because they 'knew too much.' In magic, the Joker really helps. Let me show you."*

Fan the deck and remove the Joker, setting it on the table in front of you. Give the deck a few cuts and then spread the cards so that your spectator may take one. *"Take out a single card, but do not look at it. Merely put it in your pocket."* Cut the deck at the point at which the card was removed, getting a glimpse of the bottom card as you complete the cut. This will tell you the name of the selected card (add three in value). Hand the Joker to your spectator. *"Please put this in your pocket for a moment but don't let go. Just put him in there and take him out as soon as possible."*

After this has been done, take the Joker and hold it to your ear. Pretend to hear him telling you something. For example, we will say the card selected was the Nine of Hearts. (The spectator still does not know what card he has.) *"What's that? You say the card in the gentleman's pocket is a red card? It is a Heart? Which one, please? It looks like an upside down Six? That must be a Nine. The Nine of Hearts!"* Point to the spectator dramatically. *"Please reach into your pocket and remove the Nine of Hearts."* He will do so in great amazement. *"Never underestimate the power of a Joker."*

Gambler's Wish

The system we are using lends itself to many interesting possibilities. This is a demonstration that may earn you the reputation of being a "card hustler."

Spread the deck face up on the table and announce: *"As you can see, the deck is not stacked in any way."* (This is just a white lie, but don't feel guilty.) Scoop the cards up before they have a chance to study them, but in doing so you look for any Deuce. Cut the deck at that point, so the Deuce is on the bottom. *"Combining a little magic with some good card skill,*

I'd like to show you the gambler's wish. Let's play a little four-handed poker."

Deal out four poker hands. You get the fourth hand. (If you have learned to do the false cut, do so before you start to deal.) After dealing you are ready to astound the group. Turn up the hands one at a time, beginning with the one on the far left. Each hand will have a straight flush. *"Every player's dream has come true and the betting will get rather high."* Now turn up your hand. *"But the dealer always wins."* Your hand will hold the Royal Flush.

It Must Be Mind Reading

This is probably one of the strongest effects you can do with the Stebbins system. It can be featured on a stage or in the living room just as easily. Many professional magicians do this as a mind-reading demonstration.

After cutting the deck rapidly a few times, ask one spectator in the group to come forward and to remove a *"bunch of cards"* or a *"small handful of cards from the center of the deck."* Spread the cards between your hands to make this easier. Once he has taken the cards, cut the deck, shifting the cards on top to the bottom of the deck. (These are all the cards remaining above the group he took away.) Take a look at the bottom card while you give further instructions. *"Please mix the cards thoroughly. Take one card, without looking at it, and place it in your pocket. Now hand a few cards to some of the people around you so that others can participate in this demonstration of mental concentration."*

Speak with authority, almost commanding audience attention. *"Will the people who have cards in their hands please concentrate on their cards and I shall try to receive the thoughts as you do."* The bottom card will tell you the name of the next card in sequence. Let us say, for example, that the bottom card is the Four of Clubs. Someone holds the Seven of Hearts. *"Someone is concentrating on a Heart. It is the Seven of Hearts. Does anyone have that card, please?"* Take back the card after it has been acknowledged. Place it on the bottom of your deck as a reminder. At the same time you will be setting the deck for use again. Name the next card as dramatically, pretending to concentrate: *"I see a Spade, a Ten of Spades."*

Name a few cards. At one point you will name a card and no one will acknowledge it. This is the card in the spectator's pocket. Do not mention it again but continue with the next card. However, try to remember the card because you will use it for your finale. After naming a few cards you ask, *"Does anyone else have any cards left?"* If they do, continue to name them as though reading their minds. Now you are supposedly finished. Thank the group for participating. *"You have just seen a demonstration of what some might call telepathy. This is also known as thought transference. However, there is still something called clairvoyance—knowing about something that is out of sight. For example, the gentleman placed a single card in his pocket. Even he does not know its value. I shall attempt to identify it."* Place your hand against your temple as though deep in concentration, then name the card you called earlier. *"Thank you very much."* Take a bow.

This can be the strongest trick in your act and may well be used to close your repertoire.

Clairvoyant

After using the Stebbins system it may be a good idea to shuffle the deck thoroughly or to break the sequence for the wise spectator who will want to see the deck. This effect is one that will destroy the set-up at the end. It is also a very powerful closing trick.

The deck is set and a spectator is chosen to come up to assist you. Hand him or her the deck and explain that you will give some instructions that must be followed exactly. He or she is to leave the room, taking the deck, but staying within earshot.

"Shuffle the deck in an overhand fashion. Can you do that? Once or twice will do. Now follow these instructions."

You may be surprised at the instructions but here is a simple fact: an overhand shuffle will break the sequence into small blocks but the blocks will still be in the proper sequence to do this particular trick. You will also notice that the patter is short and does not give the spectator time to react.

"Place the deck behind your back. Cut it once and replace the cut. Remove the top card. Do not look at it. Put it in your back pocket or coat pocket. You may come back into the room now, please."

After he or she returns you will go over the instructions and ask if they were followed. *"Turn the deck face up and remove any Queen. May I have it, please?"* As soon as the spectator turns the deck face up you have a chance to note the bottom card. The odds are very much in your favor that the sequence is still good. Looking for the Queen is your excuse for having the deck turned over.

Hold the Queen up to your ear, pretending to get some information. *"The lady is very helpful. She tells me you followed the instructions and that you placed the Six of Diamonds in your pocket."* (Or whatever card is next in the series.) The spectator will verify that your trick was a success.

Give the deck a good riffle shuffle.

Pre-Arranged Cards (The Stack)

♠♣♥♦ In gambling terms a "stack" is a group of cards that has been pre-arranged for a cheater to win. In magic the stack is any group of cards that has been arranged to accomplish a trick. Learn to shuffle and you can control the stack cards so that they remain intact after you have supposedly shuffled them.

Happenstance

This trick requires a "stack"—a small group of cards arranged in a specific order. This stack requires two sets of four-of-a-kind. (Example: four Tens and four Kings.) Place one set on top of the other; it makes no difference in what order.

Hand the deck to the spectator. *"Please deal four cards onto the table in a row . . . fine. Now deal another row of four, next to the first row. Thank you."* Take the deck back. *"We will discard either one of the two rows. Which shall we take away?"* Pick up the cards in the row he discards and bury them in the middle of the deck.

"There are four cards left. Please place your finger on the one you want us to keep." Remove the three discards and place them on the bottom of your deck. *"We'll leave that card alone on the table for a moment. Please cut the deck in half."* The spectator will do this. You must keep track of the bottom half. *"Please point to either half."* If he chooses the **top** half, you pick it up and point to the cards on the table. *"Fine. Please pick up the remaining cards."* If he chooses the **bottom** half, you take away the top half and give him the same instructions.

"Deal the cards into three neat piles, please." As he is dealing you will add: *"I won't touch the cards. I want you to do this all by yourself."*

When he has finished dealing out all the cards have him turn the top card of each pile face up. They will all match. *"Wouldn't it be more than a coincidence if this card we left on the table matched the others?"*

Turn it face up and wait for the applause.

He Went Down with His Ship

This deck is stacked by having all the even-numbered cards on top, with the odd-numbered cards on the bottom. Separate the two stacks with a Joker. (Consider the Jack as eleven and King as thirteen, with the odd cards. The Queen is considered even, with a value of twelve.)

Remove the stacked deck from its case and look for the Joker. You will cut the deck at that point so that you have twenty-six cards in each half, which you will ribbon-spread on the table. *"Please take a card from either spread. Look at it, remember it, and place it somewhere in the center of the other half. Shuffle the half that has your card in it. Place that on top of the deck remaining on the table."*

You will now be able to pick up the cards and by looking for the one that is out of place, find the card he chose. It will either be the only even card in the odd group, or vice versa. Put this card on top of the deck. Drop the deck into a borrowed hat. Slip the top card under the hat band and hold it there with your hand as you shake the hat. *"There's a story I read recently about a ship with forty or fifty passengers and a crew. They ran into a terrible storm. Some of them took to the life boats."* Take a bunch of cards out of the hat and drop them onto the table. Keep shaking the hat, this time a bit more violently. *"A few jumped overboard!"* Flip a bunch of cards into the air and let them fall where they may. *"Several people were saved."* Remove the few remaining cards and relax your hold on the card under the hatband so that it slides into the hat. *"Through all of this the good Captain stayed with this ship. I can't recall his name. What was the name of your card? Six of Spades* [or whatever it is]? *That was his name."* Hand the hat to the spectator and allow him to remove the card.

Wayward Jacks

Youngsters love stories. This is a card effect that lends itself nicely to a tale of sadness that has a happy ending. Stack the deck from the top card down, as follows:

Jack of Diamonds, Jack of Spades, Jack of Clubs, Queen of Clubs, Queen of Hearts, Queen of Spades, King of Spades, King of Clubs, King of Diamonds, and Queen of Diamonds. You will have ten cards, but you refer to them as nine cards throughout this trick. . . .

Lift the ten cards off the deck. *"I'm going to tell you a story using nine cards. Three little boys loved to run away and hide."* Fan the three top cards, lift them to show the Jacks, and place them on the bottom of the packet. *"Their mothers would go looking for them."* Lift the next three cards and show the Queens. Place these on the bottom. *"Their fathers would go looking for them."* Lift the next three cards and fan them to show three Kings. Push off the three top cards and square them with the right hand. Turn the cards face up for a moment so the audience gets a flash of the Jack on the bottom. (Do not let them see the other cards. Make sure they are squared neatly.) Place these three cards on the bottom. *"One day the boys really got lost. Their mothers searched the city for them."* Spread the top three cards, but do not show them. Count aloud, *"One, two, three,"* and drop them on top of the deck on the table. *"Their fathers hunted through the countryside."* Count off three more cards in a fan and drop these onto the top of the deck. *"That's six . . . and three is nine."* Drop the remaining four cards onto the deck. *"No one knew where the boys were. Do you?"* No matter what the reply, you fan three cards off the top and drop them face down on the table. Fan three more the same way.

Fan the last three and place them on the table. *"Where did you say they were?"* Wait for another guess. *"They got good and hungry and they all went back to their own homes."* Turn up the three sets and show each one to have a Jack, Queen, and King.

In the event that you do not wish to memorize the specific cards, the trick will still work but the cards will not come up in matching suits. You can stack any three Jacks, three Queens, three Kings, and an extra Queen. You'll achieve the same result.

Triple Match

Coincidences don't happen unless a magician is working. Here's a trick with a surprise ending. The three top cards of the deck should match the three bottom cards in their opposite suits. A Three of Clubs will match the Three of Spades, etc. If you have learned how to riffle shuffle you can shuffle the pack allowing the bottom cards to fall first and the top cards last. In this way the middle of the deck is shuffled but the top and bottom cards remain untouched. If you can't riffle, merely begin the trick without it.

Place the deck on the table. *"Please cut the pack in half and take either one for yourself."* You pick up the other half. *"We will both deal out the cards into three piles, like this."* Begin to deal the cards from left to right into three piles. After you have dealt a few cards you allow him to begin his dealing as you finish yours. All the cards are now dealt out. If the spectator took the top half of the deck, you will instruct him: *"Slide out the bottom card of each pack and put them in your pocket. Don't let anyone see them, not even yourself."* If he selected the bottom half, give him similar instructions; he is to *"slide off the top card of each pile, and without looking at them place them in your pocket."* You must remember which half he selected. If he used the bottom cards you will now lift each of your **top** cards. If he put his top cards in his pocket, you slide off your **bottom** cards. *"I'll do just the opposite."* Put your cards in your pocket.

"Put your hand into my pocket and pull out a card. Be careful, I'm ticklish." When he draws the card, allow him to drop it face up onto the table. Since you know the order of the cards, you can now reach into his pocket and draw the matching card. If the card you find is not a matching card, don't worry. The trick is just as surprising when the second card matches. When all three match the trick is over.

"We have three matches. You must be very careful when you carry matches in your pocket."

Stab Mental

Use a little acting and showmanship for this one and you will have your audience talking about you for days.

Set up ten cards from Ace through Ten in a descending sequence, as follows: 5-4-3-2-Ace-10-9-8-7-6. Use any suits, a few cards of each, so that they are not all the same colors. This stack is on top of your deck before you begin the trick.

Allow the spectator to cut the deck. This will bring the stack to the middle. Allowing the spectator to do this merely throws suspicion away from the possibility that you may be using a set-up deck. Fan the cards in front of you and find the ten stack, pulling it out of the deck, and placing it on the table, face down. *"We'll use a bunch of cards for this experiment in mind reading."* Fan the ten cards in front of the spectator so he can see them, and say: *"Please think of any one of the cards. You may change your mind but when you have finally selected one, please remember it."* Before putting the ten cards on top of the deck again, cut them exactly in half. (Move the five top cards to the bottom.) This will bring the Ten spot to the top of the deck.

Hand the deck back to the spectator. *"Hold the deck under the table, please. You will transfer cards from the bottom to the top of the deck. Take as many cards from the bottom as the value of the one card you thought of."* If he selected a Deuce, he will move two cards from bottom to top. If he chose a Five spot he moves five cards, etc.) *"May I have the deck when you have done this?"*

At this point you might want to be more dramatic and have yourself blindfolded. At any rate, you now have the cards, which are held in dealing position. Begin to deal them in a haphazard order around the table. As you deal you will mentally count the cards until you reach the *eleventh* card. This will be the selected card. Keep dealing, but keep track of this card. Do not lose sight of it. (If you are using a blindfold, you can look down through the space next to your nose and keep the cards close to the edge of the table.) After the cards have been dealt pretend to mix them further by moving them around on the table. Do this by placing your right thumb on the selected card and moving the others with the fingers. The card under your thumb is always in your control.

Borrow a kitchen knife and hold it above the mess of cards.

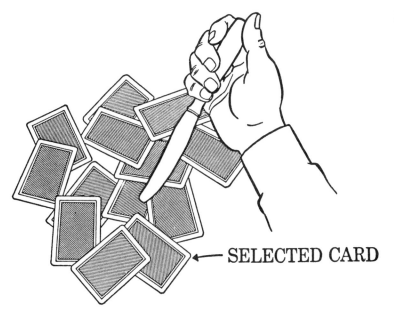

←— SELECTED CARD

Suddenly come down with the knife so that the blade lands on top of the selected card. *"This is the one you were thinking of. Please tell us what it is."* After he names the card, turn it up to show that you were correct.

Magic by Mail

Your friends or business associates will be astounded and amused by this trick, which can be done by mail. A letter must accompany the pack of cards you will send. This is how the letter reads:

"Please read these instructions very carefully. Remove the deck of cards from the case. You may examine them to make sure they are not marked or arranged in any special order. Cut the pack a few times. Now cut the pack and shuffle one half into the other. Use a riffle shuffle on the table to make sure they are mixed. Now cut the pack. Remove a single card from either half of the deck. Write down the name of this card so you won't forget it. Place the card in the center of the other half. Please mail back either half of the cards remaining."

To prepare this, take a regular deck and shuffle it thoroughly. You will now record the exact sequence. Jot the cards down in a circle as in illustration #1. You will now mail the deck and

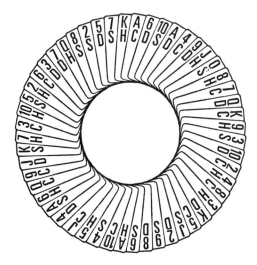

the instructions. When you get the deck back in the mail, you will record all the cards and check them off alongside your circle. You will find that there will be two groups in sequence. If a card is missing from the sequence, it was the selected card, which is still in his possession. If the card he chose was returned, it will be an isolated card that does not belong in either group you checked off. (See illustration #2.) You can then phone or mail a post card that reads: *"Your card was the Six of Spades"* (or whichever it was).

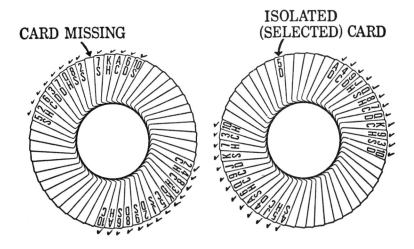

CARD MISSING

ISOLATED
(SELECTED) CARD

A Special Arrangement

You will use a stack for this trick but, so that it does not look like a special arrangement, you will pretend to take the cards out of the deck at random. Here is how to prepare the deck:

Remove all of the Spades from the deck and arrange them from the top card down, as follows: Ace-Queen-2-8-3-Jack-4-9-5-King-6-10-7.

Shuffle the remaining cards thoroughly. Now turn the deck face up and replace the Spades so that the order will not be broken. Place the Ace near the top or left-hand section of the face-up deck, the Queen next, and so on, so the cards are dispersed in the deck. The deck goes back in its case.

When you are ready for the trick, remove the deck from the case and spread the cards face up on the table. *"Fifty-two different cards. We'll need two suits."* Pick up the deck. *"You take the Hearts and I'll take the Spades."* Openly run through the face-up cards. When you come to a Heart, drop it face down in front of the spectator. When you come to a Spade drop it face down near yourself. Each Spade goes on top of the other one so that when all have been removed, the stack will remain in the original order.

"Find your Ace and see if you can follow me." Your top card is an Ace. Place it face up on the table. Duck the next to the bottom of the deck. Deal the next one face up; it is the Deuce. Continue to duck one and deal one and you will have all the cards in sequence. Naturally the spectator cannot do this since his cards are not stacked. *"If you can't do this one you'll never be able to become a magician."*

One-Way
Cards

♠♣♥♦ The description of the principle explains this title. Whenever you borrow a deck of cards look for the possibility of using it as a One-Way deck.

One-Way

Many decks of playing cards have designs, advertisements, or company logos instead of over-all patterns. If the cards are arranged with the patterns all facing in the same direction, a single card removed and reversed will stand out quite obviously. If you happen to find one of these decks, use it to its best advantage.

Have a card selected from the pack. When the spectator is looking at the card, turn the pack around so that he will replace the card with its pattern inverted. Shuffle the deck in an overhand shuffle. Face the spectator and hold the pack in front of him so he can see all the faces of the cards. *"Please concentrate on the card you chose. As soon as you see it, please think of the word 'Stop.' Do not say it aloud. Here we go."*

Spread the cards. He is looking for his card, you are looking at the back designs. As soon as you come to his card, the only one in the set that does not belong, lift up the card. *"Is this the one?"*

Miracle Deck

This is a little-known method of making any deck a one-way deck. Use a sharp pin or a needle and carefully scratch out a small section of the color in the back design. Do this on only one side of the card, at the upper left index corner.

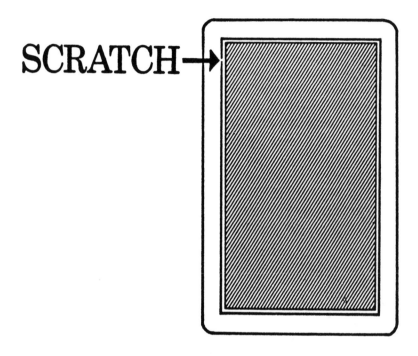

SCRATCH→

After you've done this with all the cards, the deck is now the same as a one-way deck. You can now do some "miracles" with this pack.

Remove all the Spades from the deck. Turn them around and replace them. Now you can amaze the bridge players. Start to deal cards onto the table. Each time you see your mark, set the card aside. After dealing out the deck you have removed thirteen Spades. Announce that you have just dealt a "grand slam" bridge hand.

Using the Miracle Deck

1. Reverse the four Aces and announce that *"very few people know that the factory uses less ink in printing Aces and therefore they are lighter in weight than the average card."* Pretend to weigh each card in your hand as you deal them off the deck. When you see your Aces, set them aside until you have found all four.

2. Alternate the red cards and the black cards—scratches up for black cards, down for reds. Give the deck a good riffle shuffle, making sure you don't disturb the arrangement of the backs. Hold up each card as you deal, asking the spectator to think of the color. You name it as you deal it. You can now separate the reds from the blacks without seeing the cards.

3. Cut the pack into two equal piles, but reverse one pile. Have the spectator select a card from one pile, look at it, and replace it in the other pile. Now turn the first pile around again and riffle shuffle the two together. A ribbon spread on the table will show up the selected card.

4. You can also make a "miracle deck" by preparing the face cards with a small pin scratch on one index corner. The same tricks can be used, but your locations will be from a face-up pack.

COLOR SCRATCHED

Mathematical and Self-Working Card Tricks

♠♣♥♦ This title is a broad one, but it is accurate. If you know how to count, you can do any of these at a moment's notice.

Big Ben

This is probably one of the most effective tricks you will do. Have fun with it and feel free to ad lib where you think you can get extra chuckles. You will need to know the *thirteenth* card from the bottom of the deck. Just for example, we will say it is the Ace of Spades. Before you begin the trick you will write the name of this card on a sheet of paper and place it in full view of the audience as a prediction. *"Here is a prediction of something that is going to happen. During this experiment I will ask you to keep one eye on the deck . . . one eye on me . . . and one eye on the prediction."*

Hand the deck to the spectator. *"Please turn the deck face up and place it on the table. By the way, have you ever done any traveling? Where have you been? Have you ever been to England? I'm sure you must have heard about Big Ben."* (Look into audience and pretend to have heard someone. *"No, madam—not Uncle Ben; it's Big Ben, the famous clock on the tower. Sir, will you try to picture Big Ben in your mind. Can you see it there with its large numbers? Picture an hour on the clock—one, two, three, four, or any hour at all. Have you got this picture in your mind? Good."*

So far nothing has happened and the deck is lying face up on the table. *"I will now turn my back. Please take as many cards from the face of the deck as the hour suggests. If you chose three o'clock, take three cards; six o'clock, take six cards. Have you got the idea? Put the cards in your pocket when you've taken enough."*

Turn back to face the spectator. *"You are now thinking of an hour on the clock face. We will need twelve cards to draw a picture of the clock."* Pick up the deck and deal twelve cards onto the table, one at a time. (This will reverse the order.) Place the rest of the deck aside and begin to lay out the cards in a clockwise circle, **beginning with one o'clock.** Each card will represent one hour. *"I now have a better picture of the clock. I won't ask you what time you chose, but I must know if it was morning or afternoon."* No matter what the reply, continue:

"Do you have a clear picture? That's unusual because London is generally quite foggy. Let me look at the clock." Look for the Ace of Spades. It will fall at the exact hour the spectator chose. If, for example, it sits at six o'clock, it means he has

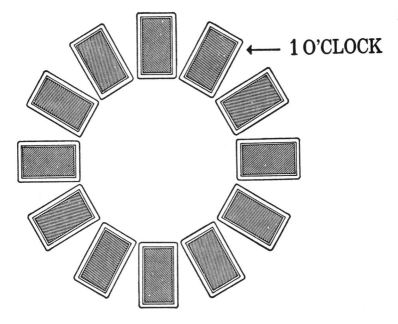

← 1 O'CLOCK

six cards in his pocket. Make the announcement as though reading his mind. *"I believe the hour you thought of was six o'clock. Is that correct? Please remove the cards from your pocket and count them onto my palm, one at a time."* At this point the trick seems to be over, but you will now make it a miracle. *"Now, will you please look at my clock on the table and see what card falls at six o'clock."* He will name the Ace of Spades. *"If you remember, before we began our experiment, I made a prediction of something that was going to happen. Please look at the prediction and read it aloud."* He will read *"THE SELECTED CARD WILL BE THE ACE OF SPADES."*

VARIATION: Should you have the opportunity to use your own deck of cards, you can add a card of contrasting color to the thirteenth position, such as a red card in a blue deck. Since all the cards are dealt face up, no one will see the odd color. When the prediction has been made and the odd card has been chosen, turn all the other cards over, showing them blue. Then turn up the red one for an additional surprise.

Time Will Tell

Magicians like to use the clock as a way to find chosen cards. This is one of many tricks possible with this principle. Use a borrowed deck and allow the spectator to shuffle it. When you take the pack, casually spread the cards between your fingers. Silently count off thirteen cards and hand them to an assistant as though you picked them off at random.

"Here, take a bunch of cards for yourself." Place the balance of the deck on the table. Turn your back.

"While my back is turned, please take some of those cards and put them in your pocket. Shuffle the rest of the cards. Now look at the bottom card and try to remember it. Put the cards back on top of the deck on the table." You can now turn around.

Pick up the deck and begin to deal out twelve cards in a *counter-clockwise* fashion. The first card you deal will be placed at the twelve o'clock position, the next card at eleven, and so on, until you have dealt a circle of cards on the table. Place the rest of the pack behind the twelve o'clock card.

FIRST CARD

"*This will represent the face of a clock.*" Make sure the spectators understand this by showing them a few cards and calling them by the hour they represent. "*This one is three o'clock, this one is six, and so on.*" Ask the spectator to remove the cards he placed in his pocket earlier. "*Please count the cards you selected. How many are there?*" (Let us assume he had five cards.) "*You selected five cards. That will represent five o'clock. Please look at the clock and put your finger on the card that falls in the five o'clock position.*" He will do this and you remove all the other cards. "*What was the name of the card you looked at earlier?*" When he names the card, allow him to turn up the card under his finger The selected card will always fall on the hour that is indicated by the number of cards in his pocket.

Rising Card

Many tricks can be done using this mathematical principle. Numbers between ten and nineteen all have two digits. When added together the total of the two digits is subtracted from the original number. The result will always be nine. Here is how we can use this.

Look through the deck and spot the ninth card from the top of the pack. Remember this card and set the deck on the table in front of your spectator.

"*I'd like you to think of any number between ten and twenty.*" Stress the word "between." "*Do you have that number? Good. Now please deal that many cards onto the table.*" Hand him the pack. "*Pick up the cards you now have on the table. We will total the digits of your original number to arrive at a single digit. For example, if you chose thirteen you would add the one and the three, giving you four. Got it?*" Make it clear in case he did not understand it the first time. "*You now have the new number. Deal that many cards back onto the deck.*" When he has done this, say: "*Please look at the top card of the pile you now hold. This was arrived at strictly by chance. Remember that card.*" He will be looking at the card that was your original ninth card. "*Please bury the card in the middle of the deck. I will not touch it. Shuffle the cards thoroughly.*"

Since you knew the name of his card all along you can reveal it any number of ways. Take the deck back and run through the cards, face up. Find his card and cut it to the top of the deck. Pretend to have trouble finding it. *"I'm afraid I'll need some outside help. We'll do it with static electricity."* Hold the deck in your left hand, thumb on the inner end and fingers on the other side. The back of the hand faces the audience. Rub the index finger of the right hand on your sleeve. The deck faces the audience. Place the index finger on top of the deck and command, *"Rise up!"* Nothing will happen. Rub the index finger some more. This time place the index finger on top of the deck, pressing the ball of the little finger against the middle of the selected card. As you raise the index finger, push the selected card up with the little finger. It will seem to rise out of the deck.

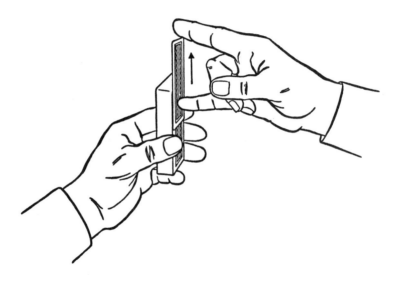

Impossible Card Location

The more people who participate in a magic effect, the more entertaining and amazing the effect can be. This effect requires three assistants.

Each spectator is requested to select a card from the shuffled pack. The deck must have all fifty-two cards and no Jokers.

"Please be sure to remember your cards as we try to lose them forever in the pack." As you talk, spread fifteen cards to your right from the top of the pack. Do not make it look as though you are counting; merely transfer the cards casually

in groups of five. Remove the fifteen cards and set them on the table to your right.

Do the same with another fifteen cards (C, below), setting them to the left of the first pile (B). Ten cards are placed to your left as pile A. You are still holding nine cards.

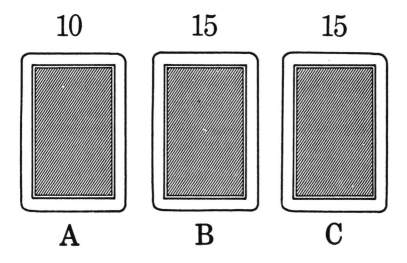

"*We'll try to make the cards impossible to find.*" Point to spectator number one and request that he "*pick up the first pile (A) and shuffle the cards thoroughly. Put the pile back on the table and place your card on top. Take a few cards from the middle pack and shuffle those. Drop them on top of your card. The card is lost.*" The second spectator shuffles pile B. "*Please mix the cards in the middle pack. Place your card on top. Now take a few cards from the last pile (C) and shuffle those. Drop them on the pile.*" Give the same instructions to the third spectator. He will shuffle pile C, then place his card on top. Now hand him your nine cards. He will shuffle them and add them to the pile.

Pick up the three piles, placing pile C on top of B. Then these cards go on top of pile A. "*The cards are lost in the pack.*" Push off four cards from the top as you speak. Cut them to the bottom.

"*I'll deal the cards into two piles. Some will be face up and some will be face down. When you see your card in a face-up pile, call 'Stop!'*" Begin to deal the first card face UP, the next card beside it, face DOWN. Add another card to the face-up pile, then another face down. Alternate the deal until you have dealt all the cards. No one will call "Stop." "*You're sure you haven't seen your cards?"* Pick up the face-down pack and repeat the process, making sure to deal the first card face up. You will repeat this process of elimination until you have only three cards left in your face-down pile. *"Only three remain. This one is yours."* Push the top card to spectator number three (the last one). The middle card was selected by spectator number two and the bottom card belongs to the first man.

The Piano Trick

Some of the old tricks are still the best tricks. This one goes back to about 1900 and is called the Piano Trick because of the position of the hands during its performance.

"You have very nice hands. Do you play the piano? Please put your hands on the table as though you were sitting at the keyboard. Let me take some cards and set them between your fingers."

Insert a pair of cards between each of the two adjacent fingers, including the thumb. Set out seven pairs like this, but the last time you will place only a single card between his left third and fourth fingers.

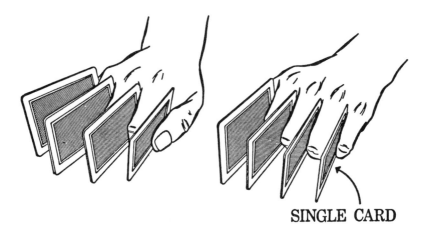

SINGLE CARD

"We have placed two cards, an EVEN number, between each of your fingers and a single ODD card here." Point to the last card. Remove the first pair of cards at your left (his right hand) and separate the two cards, placing them side by side on the

table. Do the same with the next two so that they go on top of the first two on the table, forming two piles. Repeat this until you have all the pairs. As you pair them off, make mention of it: *"Two cards here. An even number."* Pick up the single card. *"This is an ODD card. On which pile shall I place the ODD one?"* Add this to whichever pile he chooses. *"I will now try to pass the odd card to the even pile."* Pick up the pile you just used. Snap your fingers. *"There it goes. It isn't here any longer."* Deal the cards off the packet in pairs. You will have an even number. Now pick up the other pile. Deal these in pairs and you will have a single card left over.

Your Deal

This one works all by itself and will not only fool the onlooker but yourself as well. The instructions to the spectator must be clear. Your deck must have all fifty-two cards.

After he or she has shuffled the pack, request that the spectator *"cut the deck exactly in half."* This may be a bit difficult to do, so after the cut has been made, try to even them up by moving a few cards from the higher pile to the lower one. For the trick to work the cut must be within four cards of the center.

"Take a card from anywhere in either half. Please remember it and place it on top of its pile. Now cover it with the other pile so that your card is now lost in the middle of the deck. Deal the top four cards in a row on the table. Keep dealing the cards until you have four heaps." Use your finger to point to the spot on the table where you want him to deal.

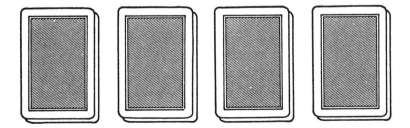

After your spectator has dealt the cards, turn up each pile so the cards can be seen. Have him or her indicate which pile contains your spectator's card. Turn that pile face down and discard the others. Hand him or her the pile indicated.

"Please deal these into four more piles." When this has been done, the last card dealt will be on pile number one. Comment: *"That pile isn't even, so we'll get rid of it."* (Discard it, leaving three piles on the table.) *"Please take the top and bottom cards of each pile and throw them onto the discard heap."* Three single cards will remain on the table. Pick them up from left to right and hand them to the spectator. Eliminate the top and bottom cards of this pile. *"Please name your card."* It is the one left in your spectator's hand.

A Process of Elimination

This one is entirely automatic. Spread the deck of cards so that your spectator can select a card. As you do this, run the cards in groups of five so that you can count them as you spread them. When the card has been removed keep counting until you get to number twenty-one. Separate your hands at that point so that you have twenty-one cards in the right hand and the balance in the left. The selected card is replaced on top of the cards in your left hand. Add the cards in the right hand and you have placed his card exactly twenty-second from the top.

"I'll deal some cards face up and some face down. Watch the face-up group. Look for your card, but don't tell me when I pass it."

Begin to deal the cards. The first card is placed face up in front of your spectator, the next card face down near you. The next one goes face up and you begin to form two piles, one face up and the next face down. His card will not appear in the face-up group. *"Have you seen your card?"* He will answer *"No."* Push the face-up cards aside and pick up the face-down cards. Repeat the process, dealing the first card face up and alternating the cards as before. *"Have you seen it in this group?"* His answer will always be *"No."* Repeating this process you will find that you can go through the entire deck without him seeing his card. The very last face-down card you will be holding is his card.

A Perfect Match

Good swindles are always a delight to perform. This one is no exception. You yourself will enjoy the outcome, although the spectator will have no conception of what has actually taken place. You'll need two assistants for this one.

After the pack has been shuffled allow each spectator to cut off a small packet of cards. *"I will turn my back while each of you count your cards."* They count silently as you turn your back. *"Either one of you may take all the cards you both hold, and shuffle them together."* When this has been done, you turn around. *"I have no way of knowing which number you each have arrived at. Please remember the numbers."* Go to the first spectator, showing him the faces of the cards. *"As I go through these cards, please count them until you come to your number. Remember the name of the card that falls at that number. You may shuffle the cards first if you like."* Pull the first card into your right hand. Now peel off the second card and place it in front of the first one, directly on its face. Take the next card in front of the second and continue to go through the cards, one at a time. You are actually reversing the order as you do this. The very last card shown goes on the bottom, or under, the face-up packet. *"You've seen a single card which falls at the number you have in mind. Will you, sir, please do the same."*

Turn to the next spectator and repeat the business of counting the cards. Do so in the same manner, one on top of the other, reversing the order. Oddly enough, **both spectators will select the same card.** Have the packet shuffled again and request that they be cut into two even piles. *"What I shall attempt to do is cause both of your cards to turn up at the very same moment. As soon as you see your card, please call 'Stop!'"* Begin to turn up the two top cards of each pile at the same time. Turn the cards face up in two new piles on the table. Both assistants will stop you at the same time. They both have the same card. You will not give them a chance to compare notes. When they stop you, point to both cards and call their names. For example, they both selected the Ten of Clubs. Two cards will turn up together. You name them. *"Here they are, gentlemen—the Ten of Clubs and the Five of Diamonds."* Each man will assume that the other one selected the Five. *"A perfect match."*

A More Perfect Match

You can vary the same tricks by changing the scenery. This effect is done exactly as you did the first version of the Perfect Match. Use an old deck of cards so you won't feel so bad about tearing them.

Use about seven or eight cards. Pick them off the top of your shuffled deck. Tear them in half in front of the spectators. *"This may not be enough. I'll need more cards."* (Tear more cards in half.) *"What's wrong? Haven't you ever seen anyone cut the deck before?"* You now have fourteen or sixteen halves. Shuffle the half pieces as you talk. Hand the packet to one of the spectators. *"Please take a bunch of these and leave some for your friend."* As in the previous trick, have them count their pieces and remember the number. You will then proceed exactly as you did before. Have each spectator look at the card that falls at the selected number. Make sure the cards are reversed in order as you show them to the first spectator. The last piece goes under the face-up packet. When both spectators have arrived at their cards, have the pieces shuffled all together. Hand the pack to the first spectator. *"Please go through these and find half of the card you looked at. Don't show us this piece; just put it on the table, face down."* After he has done this, give the same instructions to the other assistant. When the second spectator has placed his card on the table, you remark: *"Isn't that a coincidence—the pieces seem to fit."* Push them together like a puzzle. *"That's a perfect match. Here's a more perfect match."* Turn both halves face up and they will see that they have selected the same card.

Back Where We Began

It is very intriguing when the magician takes the cards behind his back or under the table. The spectator always wonders what is going on. You can always answer, *"The reason I do this behind my back is because what I must do . . . is none of your business."*

The spectator is requested to think of any number between one and ten. *"Look through the deck and remember the name of the card that is resting at that number. If you pick number three you will remember the third card. Leave the card there, but remember it."* Once this has been done you offer more instruction. *"Now you have a number and a card. Take as many cards from the bottom of the deck as the number you selected, and put them on top. If you had number three, take three cards from the bottom and put them on top."* Take the deck from him. *"Remember the card and the original number while I do some fancy arranging."* Take the deck behind your back, or under the table. Here's what you do. Push the top card forward. Push the next card below the top card. The next card goes forward. Repeat this, alternating the action until you have moved twenty cards in all.

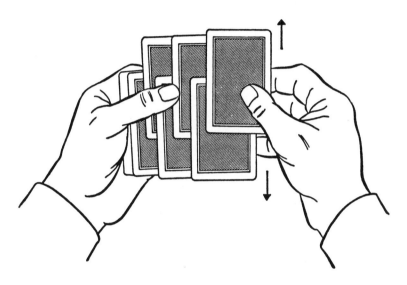

Ten cards are now extending over the front of the deck. Pull these out and place them on the bottom of the deck. The selected card will now be back in the same position it was when your spectator began the trick. *"What number was your card at originally? Count them, please, and you'll see it is back where it started."*

Predicto

Make sure you are using a full deck of fifty-two cards for this one. Remove the Jokers. Allow the onlooker to shuffle the deck. Square it up neatly but steal a peek at the bottom card before you set the pack on the table. Write the name of the bottom card on a piece of paper and fold it carefully, so that no one can see it. *"This is a prediction of something that is going to happen later."* Put it in a place where all can see it.

Instruct the spectator: *"Please deal out a dozen cards from the top of the deck."* When he has done this, spread the cards around the table rather haphazardly. *"Choose any four of these, please."* Remove the rest of the cards and place them on the bottom of the deck. *"You may turn the four cards face up. I will deal cards below each one so that we will have a total of ten for each card."* (Example: He turns up a Four, Seven, Ten, and Queen. Start with the Four and deal out enough cards to total ten, or six more cards.) *"Four. Five,"* (deal one) *"six,"* (another) *"seven,"* (keep dealing cards) *"eight, nine, and ten."* Do the same with the Seven. Call *"Seven"* and deal numbers *"eight, nine, and ten"* (three cards). The court or face cards will count as Ten, so no cards will be dealt for these. Do this for all four cards.

Keep the original cards on the table, but discard the cards you just dealt. Put them on the bottom of the deck. *"Please total the values of the four cards."* He will arrive at a total (thirty-one in the example). Remove the four cards, placing them on the bottom of the deck. Hand him the deck.

"Please count to the number you have just reached by your addition." He will count to the proper number and the last card he deals is turned face up. Now ask someone to read your prediction. It will be the same as the selected card.

To make it more interesting, your prediction can read as follows:

"During the course of this performance someone will total the value of four cards and will arrive at the NINE OF HEARTS."

The One in the Middle

This one works all by itself. Just give the spectator his instructions and you will discover his selected card. Have him deal fifteen cards onto the table in three rows of five cards each. *"Pick up any pile and look at one of those cards. Remember it and shuffle your pack."* Have him place his pack on top of one of the others. Cover it with the last pile. This puts his cards in the middle of the other two groups. *"Please deal out five piles of three cards each."* This is done as though he were dealing a game — one card to each of five players, then the second cards, and finally the third. Turn up the cards in all five rows. *"Which row has your card?"* No matter which he points to it will be the middle card in that row. To make it more interesting, hand him your business card. On the back you have written *"It's the card in the middle."*

Instant Separation

Have an assistant deal two piles of ten cards each. He will turn one pile face up and the other face down. *"Please shuffle the face-up cards into the face-down cards."* Allow him to shuffle again if he wishes. *"May I have the cards behind my back, please?"* Behind your back you quickly count ten cards off the top into your right hand. The cards remaining in the left hand are turned over and you bring both hands forward, dropping each pile onto the table. *"Each packet contains the same number of face-up cards."* Spread the cards so that they may be counted. *"I'll do it again."* Scoop up the cards in the right-hand pile and turn them over on top of the cards on the left. Hand them to the spectator to shuffle. You can now repeat the trick and will end up with a different number of face-up cards. Don't repeat it more than once.

Duck One, Drop Two

A puzzle often breaks up the routine to change the pace. This one fits that description.

Openly remove ten cards of one suit, Ace through Ten. Arrange them in sequence with the Ace on top and the Ten on the bottom.

"This is a little game. I will deal the cards onto the table, one at a time. As I lift each card you will tell me whether to deal or duck a card. Each time I duck a card I will drop it on the table with the next one. I'll show you how it works. Are you ready?"

Begin to deal the cards, one on top of the other, until you are told to "duck." Take the card you would have dealt and slip it directly under the very next top card. Lift both of them off the deck and drop them onto the cards on the table.

Continue to duck one and drop two, or deal as the spectator requests. When finished, pick up the cards on the table and go through the procedure again. When you have done this twice, you will ask: *"Shall we do it once more or are you satisfied that the cards are arranged kind of crazily by now?"* No matter what the reply, you announce: *"I think we ought to check."* Turn all the cards face up. They are still in their original sequence. There is nothing more to learn; the trick works by itself. Don't let the spectator try it or it will work for him, too. Go on to your next trick.

A Card at Any Number

A working knowledge of arithmetic is essential if you want to do card tricks. This trick is a lesson in subtraction.

After the deck has been shuffled and a card has been selected, you have it replaced and find it by using your key card. When you find the selected card, cut the deck so that it is on the bottom. Say to a spectator: *"Please give me any number between twenty and forty."*

Let's assume he answers: "thirty-five." You will now subtract this number from fifty-two. (We are using a complete deck without the Joker.) This gives you seventeen. You must now add seventeen cards from the top to the bottom of the deck. In doing this you will try not to make it obvious that you are counting the cards, so talk as you explain: *"I want you to deal the cards onto the table one at a time, as I am doing."* Deal the cards singly, counting them silently as you go. *"Don't pull off a bunch like this."* Pull off a counted group to make the counting go quicker. Drop the cards onto the table. *"One at a time. Got the idea?"* Deal the rest of the cards you need for seventeen. Drop the deck on top of the cards on the table. *"What was your number again? Thirty-five? Okay, deal thirty-five cards onto the table and look at the last card."* It will be the card he chose. Always subtract the number called from fifty-two and shift the difference from the top to the bottom while you are explaining the trick.

I've Got Your Number

The Ace of Spades will act as a key card in this trick. Cut it to the bottom of the deck before you begin. Pick up the deck and spread the cards facing you, as though you are looking for the Joker. Beginning with the Ace, count twenty cards. Cut the deck at that point and the Ace will now be located twenty cards down from the top of the deck. Place the deck on the table.

"Please cut a small number of cards from the top of the deck and place them in your pocket. Now look at the top card of the deck. Please remember it. Cut the deck and lose it in the middle."

You will now pick up the cards and fan them toward yourself. Find the Ace of Spades and cut the deck so that it is now the bottom card. Beginning with the Ace start counting back again, but this time to nineteen. Cut the deck, placing the nineteen cards on top of the deck. Say: *"You took a few cards from the deck and placed them in your pocket. Neither one of us has any idea how many. You looked at a card and buried it in the middle of the deck. I believe I have located your card. Please remove the cards from your pocket and tell us how many there are."* When he does this, ask him to *"count that many cards by dealing them off the deck. The card at that number will be the card you selected."*

When this is being performed make sure that the number he cuts is less than twenty.

Gags, Bets, and Stunts

♠♣♥♦ A few of these are great to break up a routine and diversify the types of tricks you are doing. These are especially good for close-up and intimate situations.

You're Sitting on It

Your spectator should be seated for this one. Have him select a card and you find it and get it to the top of your deck. Do this with a key card to save time. Invite three other spectators to help you. *"Each of you will please take a single card. Do not look at it. Place it here on the floor."* Point your toe to a spot in front of the spectator, but just out of his reach when he bends over. The deck is still in your hand, with his card on top. *"One of those cards will change into your card. Pick up any one and put it on your lap."* As he leans forward to reach for the card, drop the top card of the pack behind him. A push with your thumb will be enough. It should fall on his chair and when he sits down again he will be sitting on the card.

"Is that your card?" He will say, *"No."* *"Give me another chance."* Hand him the deck and have him place it on his knee. *"Slap the top of the deck and your card will jump to the bottom. Go!"* He does this—also to no avail. *"Place the deck on your head and this time I guarantee your card will go to the bottom."* Tap the top card. *"That's it, your card just went down to the bottom."* He will look at the bottom card. *"No? I guess I hit it too hard. It went further down. Please stand up. You're sitting on it."*

Just by a Hair

This relevation should be done frivolously. You can find the spectator's selected card by using a key or a force. The presentation of this miracle depends upon the way you will find the card. You must get it to the top of the deck. The easiest way is to cut the deck when you have located it.

The top card is the selected card. The deck is held in the left hand, horizontally. The faces of the cards are toward the palm. The thumb is on the top card, the rest of the deck lying along the index and middle fingers of the hand.

"Many magicians pull rabbits out of hats. I use a hair myself." Pretend to pull a hair from the nearest spectator's head. *"I'll just attach the hair with a simple knot and we can pull the card out of the deck."*

Press the imaginary hair to the upper right-hand corner of

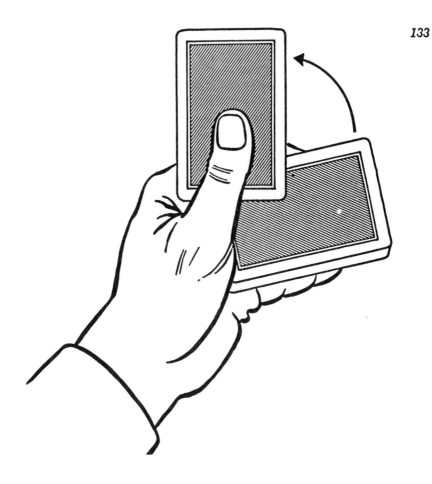

the pack, and pretend to tie a knot. Now lift the right hand about three inches away from the deck. Pretend to tug at the end of the hair, at the same time pushing the top card up and to the left with the left thumb. It will appear as though the thread is pulling the card.

Slap It!

Another interesting way to disclose the selected card is as follows: Cut the selected card to the bottom of the deck once you have found it. Now hand the deck to the spectator, asking him to hold it between his thumb and index finger. *"You remember the name of your card, which is lost somewhere in the deck. Perhaps you'll help me find it. Take a deep breath. Exhale. Fine."* At this moment strike the opposite end of the deck sharply with your index and middle fingers. The cards in his hand, with the exception of the single selected card, will fall to the floor.

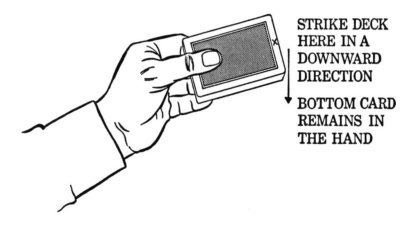

STRIKE DECK
HERE IN A
DOWNWARD
DIRECTION

BOTTOM CARD
REMAINS IN
THE HAND

Ninety-Nine Percent

We don't know how this works nor the odds on why it works, but we've done it and it rarely misfires. You can do this trick as a bet or a card trick.

Have the deck shuffled thoroughly. Do not use a new pack or one that has just been used in a game. You need a good shuffle. Place the pack on the table and announce: *"I will ask you to name two cards—just the values, not the suits. I shall attempt to place the two cards together in the pack by a snap of my finger. What are your two choices?"* (Example: a Seven and a King.) Snap your fingers above the deck and add, *"If I miss they will be no more than a single card apart."*

Start to deal the cards one at a time, face up, until you hit the two cards which will be together ninety-nine percent of the time (or within a single card apart.) If you don't see the cards together immediately, don't despair, deal out the rest of the deck. The cards called should not be in immediate sequence, such as a Six and Seven. You can add, *"Make the difference greater,"* although it works with sequence cards most of the time. Try it yourself. It's fun.

A Quarter Bet

Every deck of cards should contain a small statement that reads: "Caution, too many card tricks may be hazardous to the health of the audience." Keeping this in mind, try to select your best few tricks and stop after a reasonable period of time. Here is a stunt to help keep your evening entertaining.

Balance a playing card on the tip of your index figer. Place a quarter on the card, directly over the ball of the finger. *"I'm willing to bet that I can remove the card without touching the coin or dropping it."* Allow the spectator to try it a few times for himself before doing it for him.

To accomplish this, the middle finger of the right hand flicks the edge of the card. This propels the card, which flies away, leaving the coin balanced on the finger. It is easier to do than you imagine.

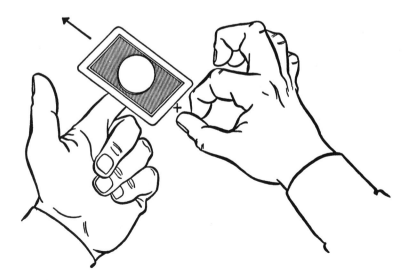

Six-Card Lift

Spread six cards on the table, face down. You will bet that by lifting only one card by its edges you can lift all six cards, so that their faces can be seen all at once. After a few people try and fail, arrange the cards as in the illustration.

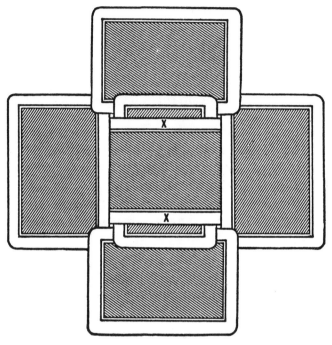

LIFT AT POINTS MARKED X

Place a single card face down vertically in front of you. The next card is placed on top of this one, horizontally (criss-cross). The other four cards are tucked or woven as follows. The next two cards are placed horizontally, one in front and one behind the first master card. They are now tucked under the master card. The last two are arranged vertically alongside the crossed card. These are then tucked under the horizontal cards and on top of the crossed card. Pick up the crossed card by its edges and you can turn the whole works over to show the faces.

Four Fives Are Sixteen

Challenge the spectator to take the four fives and arrange them so that their spots total sixteen. After a few futile tries, you demonstrate how it should be done by arranging the cards on the table this way:

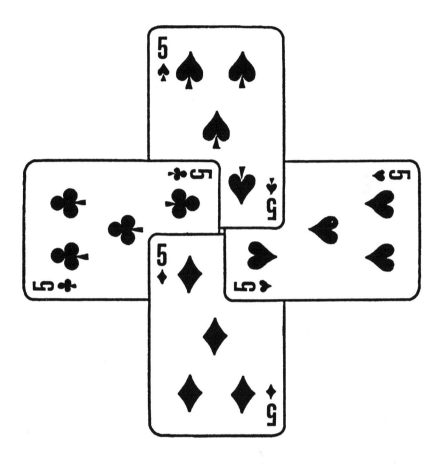

Card in Cigarette

In every large group you may meet one Mr. Know-it-all who believes nothing and needs special attention. The best way to handle a heckler is to ignore him. Only experienced comedians and entertainers can spar with them, so don't bother. However, if one gets too annoying you might bring him into the act with this gag if you see that he is a smoker.

"You seem to know a good deal about card magic. Perhaps you can help me. Do you have a pack of cigarettes? Please keep the pack in full view so that I do not touch it at any time. Take a card." Offer the pack for him to select one. *"Please put it back by yourself so that I will not be accused of manipulating the cards."* Take the cards back. *"Now I will ask you to remove any cigarette from the pack and set it down on the table. I will attempt to cause your card to leave the deck and appear rolled in the cigarette."* Snap the deck. Pick up the cigarette and hand it to him. *"Please tear it gently along the seam."* Of course nothing is there except tobacco. You have failed. *"I can't see why it isn't there."* Pick up his cigarettes and start to tear them apart, one by one. Each time you destroy another one, mutter, *"Not here either. Something is wrong. Maybe it's in this one. . . ."* The laughs will build when they see you tearing up his cigarettes. Hand him the remainder of the pack. *"Maybe I should do a few more card tricks. While I'm doing them, you might take the pack to the back of the room and check the rest yourself."*

Don't be vindictive. You are playing for laughs, not to make the man angry.

Card
Miracles

♠♣♥♦ Your strongest tricks are the best ones to use when closing your act. That's why we've saved these for last. They are very strong effects, truly Card Miracles.

Satan's Ashes

For parties and small gatherings this is a startling effect that will long be remembered. Steal into the lavatory at the first opportunity and find a small bar of soap. This prop will make you seem like the Devil's apprentice.

Dampen a corner of the soap. Pull back your sleeve and write the name of a card on your arm just above the wrist. Pick a simple card such as the Ace of Clubs so that you have room to write clearly. This will leave a soap film on your arm when it dries. Roll down your sleeve and you're ready for the show.

Your Ace of Clubs must be on top of the deck when you're ready to present the effect. *"May I borrow a handkerchief? Thank you."* Shake the handkerchief to show that it is empty. *"Will you place it over the pack, please?"* As soon as the deck is under the handkerchief, turn it upside down, the bottom card facing up. *"Please cut the deck anywhere at all so that we can find a card at random."*

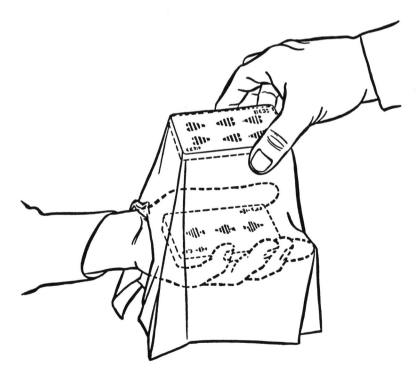

As soon as he lifts the portion under the cloth, turn your cards over again and bring them out front, offering him the top card (push it off with your thumb). *"This is the card you cut to."* Take the handkerchief from the spectator and remove the cards, turning them the right way as you replace them on the pack. Hand the spectator a small piece of paper. *"Please write the name of your card on this paper and fold it so we cannot see it."* (You already know he has the Ace of Clubs.) He will return the card to the deck himself. Place the paper in an ashtray and have someone light it so that it burns to an ash. *"This trick was taught to me by the Devil himself."* Pull back your sleeve and pick up the ashes, crumbling them into a powder. *"Please tell us the name of your card."* As he does, rub the ashes on your arm. The soap will pick up the black ash. The name of his card will be written in black on your arm.

Jack Be Nimble

During the course of your card tricks secretly slip four Jacks to the bottom of your deck. Cut a few sections of cards from the middle and place them on top. It looks as though you are mixing the cards. Place the deck on the palm of your hand.

"Please cut about half the deck and place those cards behind your back." You do the same with your half as you talk. *"Give me any one of your cards and I'll give you one of mine."* Pull a Jack from the bottom of your pile and hand it to him face down. *"Take this card behind your back and put it in your pack, but turn it upside down before you push it in."*

You take his card and merely put it on top of your deck. Then take another Jack from the bottom, turn it face up, and push it into the middle of your pack.

"Let's do this again with another card." Repeat the instruc-

tions, so that he takes your third Jack and pushes it into his pack upside down. You take your own bottom Jack and do the same in your pack.

"Now we'll see something very strange. Bring your cards out where we can all see them." Spread each packet and you will find the four Jacks reversed, two in his deck and two in yours.

You can follow this with Jack-Ro-Batics to make up an interesting routine.

Jack-Ro-Batics

The principle involved here is known to magicians as the "elevator," since cards rise mysteriously from the bottom of the pack. We will use four Jacks. You can remove them from the face-up pack quite openly.

Place all four Jacks on the bottom of your face-up pack. Show the cards and announce: *"We're going to show you some fancy acrobatics with four Jacks."* As you remove the four cards, take along one extra card from the pack. Square them all together. Put the deck on the table, face down. Hold the five cards as shown in the illustration. Your right thumb is at the inner end of the cards, the index and middle finger at the outer end. All five cards are held in the right hand.

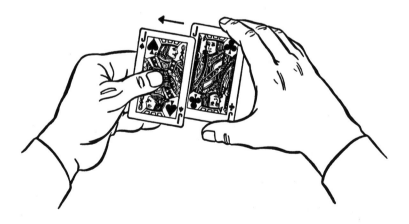

Using the left thumb, pull the first Jack into your left palm.
Pull off the second and third Jacks the same way. The last Jack has a card hidden underneath it. This is placed on top of the others in the left hand. It will look as though you have only four cards. Talk as you show the Jacks. *"These are the four circus Jacks who came from Europe a short while ago to entertain us this afternoon."* Turn the cards face down and set them on top of the deck on the table.

Now deal the top four cards in a row on the table, left to right. Three cards will be Jacks, but the card at the right end is not. The last Jack really remains on top of the deck.

"Our first Jack will perform the elevator move. He will pass rapidly through the deck." Drop the entire deck on the first card at your left. Place your index finger in the center of the deck and riffle the cards upward with the thumb and middle fingers. Snap the top card as you lift it from the deck. Show that it is a Jack and drop it face up onto the table.

Pick up the second Jack and place it on top of the deck. *"This next Jack will perform the Invisible Diving routine, passing through the deck and landing on the bottom without a net."* Riffle the cards as before. Now turn the entire pack upside down and show a Jack on the bottom. Remove it and place it next to the other face-up card.

"Jack number three will do a double-somersault and turnover." Place the third Jack face down into the face-up pack. Riffle the cards and turn the deck face down again. Deal off the top card and show it to be a Jack. Set it aside with the others. Pick up the last card. (It is not really a Jack.)

"Our last acrobatic Jack will attempt to turn himself inside out. May we have a drumroll, please." Place the last card face down in the center of the face-down deck. Riffle the edges of the cards. Spread the cards ribbon-fashion across the table. A Jack is seen face up in the center. *"May we please have some applause for these fine acrobats . . . and one more time for the magician!"* Take your bow.

It's in the Bag

Having a spectator select a card, then going through the deck to find it, can be boring. To make your revelations interesting you need dramatic or comedy touches. You want your magic to be special, not ". . . just another card trick."

Find your spectator's selected card using a key card as described earlier in this book. Bring the selected card to the top by cutting to your key card. Place the pack of cards back in its case. Close the case, but make sure the flap goes between the top card and the rest of the deck. In this way the top card may be pulled out of the deck easily. *"May I borrow a paper bag? Thank you. I believe I have the name of your card. As a matter of fact this trick is in the bag."*

FLAP GOES BEHIND SINGLE TOP CARD

Hold the bag in the right hand between the index and middle fingers. Bring the right hand to the left to take the deck. Take it with the thumb of the right hand, so that the thumb goes directly over the little notch on the flap side of the deck. Hold back the top card as you allow the deck to fall into the bag. The single card will come out under your thumb. You can now let it drop into the bag as you shake it a few times.

"What was the name of your card?" After he names it, reach into the bag and remove the deck. Hand him the bag and ask him to remove the contents. All that remains is a single card. His card.

That's the Spirit

This one is a perfect dinner-table trick. Before beginning the trick spinkle a tiny bit of salt on the table near your right hand. Have the deck shuffled in the meantime.

"You shuffle the deck and I won't touch it. For this miracle we're going to use some of the floating spirits in the room. Please cut the deck somewhere in the center. Look at the top card of the bottom section. Remember it and put it back."

As you are talking, your right index finger presses down on top of the salt on the table. Some of it will adhere to the ball of your finger. After the card has been returned to the pack, use your right index finger to point to the top of the card. Come over the card, do not touch it, but allow a few grains of salt to fall on top of the card. A shake of the hand or help with your right thumb will do this. Do not make it obvious. It should merely look as though you were given instructions. *"Replace the cut so that the cards are back where they were before you cut the deck."*

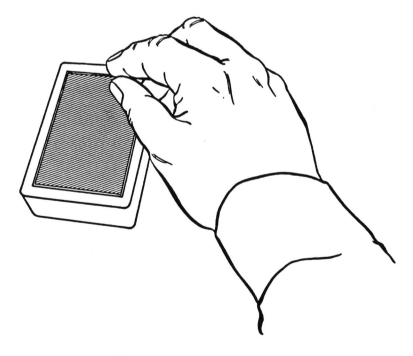

146   You will now pick up the deck and place it in the spectator's hand. His palm will be flat with the deck lying face down in the center. *"We will now ask some of the spirits to give us some help."* Hold his elbow in the palm of your hand. *"Rotate your hand a bit, please, so the spirits can find the card."* As you say this, give his elbow a gentle push. The deck will separate at the selected card. Pick up the top card and show it to verify that it is the selected card.

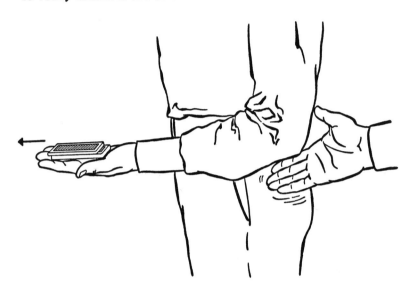

Kick It*

This is a variation of the "That's-the-Spirit" effect. The salt can be in your pocket if you're not at the dinner table. Repeat all the steps for the selection of the card and the gesture where you add the salt grains. Here is where the trick differs:

"The card is now lost in the center of the deck. Now I shall attempt some sleight of foot. Please place the deck on the floor. I have a very talented big toe. Watch!"

The side of the foot strikes the deck with a sharp blow and the cards will separate at the exact spot, finding the selected card. Have it verified.

---

* The secret of this trick was once sold for $100.

Four-Card Index

Using this simple principle you can identify any selected card, or even one that the spectator was only thinking about.

Arrange the following four cards in numerical sequence with the Ace on top: Ace of Diamonds, Two of Spades, Four of Hearts and Eight of Clubs. These are left in your pocket.

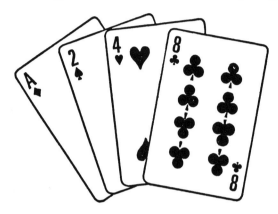

You can have a card selected from the shuffled pack or have the spectator merely think of one. Shuffle the pack and place it in your pocket directly under the four cards you have secretly placed there. In this way the four cards will be on top of the deck and within easy reach.

"I will attempt to reach into my pocket and remove a few cards that will numerically match the card you chose both in value and suit. Please name your card."

Spectator's card	Remove the following from your pocket
Six of Clubs	The Four and the Deuce for value. The Eight of Clubs for suit.
Jack of Spades	(Eleven in value.) Pull out the Two of Spades first. *"There is the Spade. That's Two. Add eight is ten, and one (Ace) is eleven."*
Ace of Clubs	*"There's the Club (Eight) and here is the Ace."*

No matter what card is named, you can make up the combination using the four cards we selected. The chart at the bottom of page 148 shows a few combinations you can put together:

You can make up all combinations using the four cards. Stop for a moment to think before reaching into the pocket. In the rare case when someone is thinking of the card that happens to be one of your four cards, you have a real miracle on your hands.

'Tis Amazing

This is a bold, perplexing "quickie" to include in your evening's entertainment. Have the deck shuffled and secretly look at the top card. Place the deck squarely on the palm of your hand, close to the thumb. Allow the spectator to cut the pack in half, placing the top half next to the other one.

TOP CARD
KNOWN TO YOU

The half closest to the spectator (B) has the "known" card. Look at the card on top of the half nearest to you (A). *"By looking at this card, I can tell you the name of the card on top of the other pile."* Remember the card you just saw and call out the name of the first "glimpsed" card. Show it to the audience.

Complete the cut by taking the half nearest you and placing it on top of the other one. You now know the name of the top card and can repeat the trick. Do this once or twice more, each time looking at the card nearest you (A) and naming the top card of the other pile (B).

The last time you do this announce: *"I will now name the top cards of both piles."* Take the top card of packet "A" and call it, naming the glimpsed card. Do not show it, but lift it off the deck so you can see it. *"And this card is the"* (name of the card you just lifted), point to the card on top of packet "B," lift the card off the deck, and drop both of them face up on the table. The audience has no idea that these were miscalled.

Chinese Card Mystery

Boldness can often produce great results for you, especially if you have already astounded your victim with a few other tricks.

Hold the deck in your left hand, your thumb at the upper left corner. Riffle the cards and ask the spectator to say *"Stop"* any time he likes. The right hand takes away the cards above the point where he stopped you. Turn the left wrist over so the deck is face up. Slide the top card (right under your thumb) to your right. You will be able to get a quick peek at the card. Turn your head away at that moment.

"Look at the card you stopped at; don't let me see it." Turn the deck face down again and add the top cards, allowing the spectator to shuffle them.

Reach into your pocket and remove a piece of paper bearing only a bunch of Chinese characters. You can clip these from a Chinese newspaper. Hand him the paper. *"Here is the name of your card. What's that? You don't understand Chinese? You're lucky I'm here. Let me translate."* (Pretend to read.) *"The name of your card is the Six of Clubs"* (or whatever card you spotted). *"Perhaps I'll do another trick in English."* Follow with another trick.

Houdini's Card

Everyone knows about Harry Houdini, the world's greatest escape artist. Although he died in 1926 he is still the most famous in his field. Mention of his name brings magic to one's mind. We're sure he wouldn't mind the mention of his name in our routine.

As you toy with the deck remove the two black Kings. *"I must tell you the story about Harry Houdini, who was a famous magician and best known for his escape tricks. It was said that no jail could hold him. He even offered rewards if they found a prison from which he could not escape. Let me show you an example of one of his escape tricks. Since I don't use ropes, chains, and locks, I will use a playing card. Please select one playing card to represent Harry Houdini."*

Allow the spectator to select a card. *"The two Kings here on the table will represent the guards at a famous prison."* Turn them face down on the table. Name the card the spectator is holding. *"This card shall be Houdini. We'll place it between the two guards, so that they can keep an eye on him."* Fan the cards of the pack as you explain: *"This will be his prison cell."* Pick up one of the Kings and insert it into the center of the pack, allowing it to protrude about half its length. Now pick up the Houdini card and place it in the deck the same way, but one card higher up in the fan. This will leave a single card between the two you just put in. The last King is placed in the deck the same way, but leaving one card between it and the selected card. (See illustration.) Close the

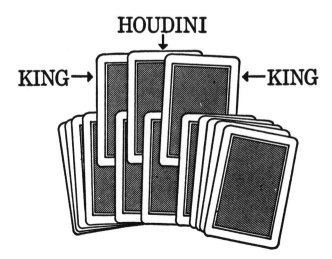

HOUDINI

KING→   ←KING

fan, allowing the three cards to protrude. *"The cell door was closed, with Houdini safely locked in between two guards."* Square the bottom of the pack. Pick up the card case with your other hand. Slip the deck halfway into the case. Hold the cards through the case by exerting pressure with your fingers along the sides of the pack. With your forefinger push the three protruding cards into the pack so that they are flush with the top of the cards. *"Into the jail they go."* Leave the flap open.

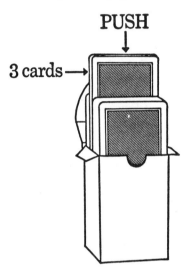

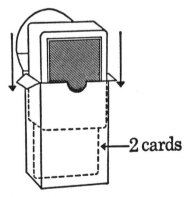

AS DECK DROPS
EXTENDED CARDS PUSH UP
SELECTED CARD

"What was the name of the Houdini card, please?" When he names it, release the deck so that it slides down into the case. The selected card will pop into view by itself. *"Here comes Houdini. He has escaped once again."*

Royal Wedding

The court cards are always the most interesting to work with. For this effect you will need the four Kings and the four Queens. As you take them out of the deck make sure that the order of the suits is the same as you put them in two piles on the table. If the four Kings run Spade, Heart, Diamond, and Clubs, arrange the Queens the same way. You can do this without fanfare as you put the cards down.

"Have you ever gone to a double wedding? Today we'll see four of them. Four Kings in one pile," (show them) *"and four Queens in the other."* Put one pile on top of the other and hand the cards to someone near you. *"Please cut the cards a few times. Thank you."* Take the cards back. *"You've mixed them up a bit. And now for the wedding, making sure the couples are evenly matched."* (Cutting will not disturb the suits.)

Place the cards behind your back. Divide the pack in half with four cards in each hand. Bring both hands out together and toss the top cards of each hand onto the table. Bring the hands behind your back each time, coming out again in a sweeping motion until there are four pairs of cards on the table. They will all match in suit, with a King and Queen as each pair. *"The right man has found the right lady. Or was it the other way around?"*

Pick up the four pairs (they are now alternating in sequence —King, Queen, King, Queen, etc.) Allow the spectator to cut them a few times. Place the cards behind your back again. This time run the cards from your left hand to your right hand, one at a time. Push the first card up a bit and the next one down about half the length of the first one. Repeat this with the four pairs. The cards are interlaced, four projecting upward and four downward.

Pull the two groups apart, stripping out the four top cards. Hold one group in each hand and bring your hands out in front of you.

"*I'm only a magician and not a minister, so I really can't perform marriages. So let's go back to where we started.*" Turn up the cards and drop them onto the table face up, showing the Kings in one pile and the Queens in the other.

The Torn & Restored Card

Traditional magicians always include one "restoration" trick in their evening's program. This is always a most startling and applause-winning effect. Something is destroyed by cutting or tearing and then it is magically restored to its original form. This is a restoration. We suggest you use an old deck because it is necessary to tear a card.

Use the Joker if you have one. Tear off the upper right-hand quarter of the card. (Diagram 1.) Discard the extra piece and place this card on the bottom of your deck before the trick begins.

Diagram 1   *Diagram 2*

Spread the cards and allow your spectator to select any card. *"This is going to be your card. In fact you may keep it after we're through with our magic. May I see it, please?"* Take the card and tear off a quarter. This will be the *index* quarter, as shown in Diagram 2. (The upper left corner of the face-up card.) Hand him this piece. *"You may hold on to that piece as a receipt."* The rest of the torn card is placed on the bottom of the pack and you turn the pack face up. *"Please put your initials or some identifying mark on the face of the card."* You hold the pack while he does this. The Joker is seen through the torn side. After he signs the card, turn your deck face down. The deck is held in your left hand as in Diagram 3.

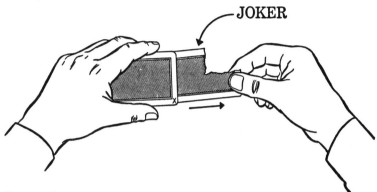

Diagram 3

Your right index finger goes under the deck at the upper right side of the pack (marked "X") and you slide the card out. This is actually the Joker. The spectator sees only a torn corner and assumes it is the same card. Leave the Joker on the table, face down. Cut the deck and set it aside for later.

You will now pick up the card on the table. Hold it so that the back faces the audience. Tear it into the three remaining quarters. Tear the quarters in half once more. Light a match or use a cigarette lighter to ignite the torn pieces over an ashtray. Do not let any of the faces be seen. As they burn, drop them into the tray. Be sure the fire is out and all trace of the printing has been obliterated.

"Do you still have the receipt I gave you? Good! Please don't lose it. Will someone take the deck and hold it tightly?" Make a magical pass or a mysterious gesture. Sprinkle some ash from the tray onto the back of the spectator's hand.

"Will the gentleman holding the deck please cut it somewhere in the center." Due to the fact that there is a missing

piece the deck will have a natural air break and the spectator should cut to the card. It is matched with the torn corner the first spectator is holding. *"And if you will, please verify the signature to make sure it is yours."*

The trick is complete and we guarantee that the next time you see these people they will request the "torn-card" trick. *ALTERNATE METHOD:* To make the pieces vanish (instead of burning them) you can push them up into the space at the upper part of your pants pocket (up toward the belt). By pulling the pocket inside out, the pieces will be hidden.

Turn-About

This is a baffling effect that is startling and mind-boggling. Look at the bottom card of the deck, remember it, and reverse it so that it is face up under the face-down pack. Spread the top cards so that your spectator can see them; then square them up again. (We will assume the card you reversed is the King of Spades.)

"Please cut off about half of the pack. Shuffle your cards. Pull one card out of the center, look at it, and remember it." You also go through the motions of pulling a card from the center, but disregard it.

"I'll place my card in your half." Push your card into the center of his pack. At the same time drop your hand to your side so that the deck is out of sight for a moment. Turn it over so that the reversed card will be on top of the deck when you bring your hand up again.

"May I have your card?" When he gives it to you, push it into your packet, face down. (The packet is really face up with the exception of the top card.) *"Now please give me half of your deck. I'll turn this over and place it on top of these cards."* Reverse his card and place them on your pack so that about one third of your cards are protruding from the back. *"May I have the rest of your cards?"* Turn these upside down and place them behind your stack so that another third is showing. It should look like the illustration.

Now push all the cards together into a single pile. It will appear that some are upside down, while others are not. *"I shall attempt to turn all the cards over so that they face in one direction. I will also cause my card and your card to reverse themselves in the pack. My card was the King of Spades* (name the card you originally reversed). *What was yours?"* After he has named the card, spread all the cards in a ribbon across the table. They will be face down, except for the two cards — your reversed card and his chosen card.

The audience will give you credit for great skill and ability after viewing this one.

Card
Handling

♠♣♥♦ Your tools are important when you build or create your magic. Just as tools are used in any other field, these are invaluable to performing and doing a better job.

Card Handling

The tricks in this book are all easy to perform and can be done with a minimum of practice. We hope that once you have had a taste of doing "miracles" with a deck you will learn some sleight-of-hand. If you are awkward in handling your cards, you will not command the full respect of your audience, so we suggest here that you learn some basics. Once you pick up a deck of cards it should look as though you are a master magician and have been handling cards all your life. After you've had a taste of applause, come back to this section and learn a few of the polishing touches.

Spreading a Deck of Cards

Most card tricks are of the "pick-a-card" variety, although we dress them in modern clothes. In having the spectator select a card you should be able to acquit yourself with the proper method of *holding* the cards.

Hold the deck face down in the left hand, as if you were ready to deal. Start pushing the cards to the right with your thumb. Your right hand comes under the deck palm up, like a tray, ready to receive the cards you just pushed away. The right thumb holds the top card while the right fingers, under the pack, pull the cards into the palm. This moves the cards from left to right in an orderly, even fashion and allows the spectator a choice of cards.

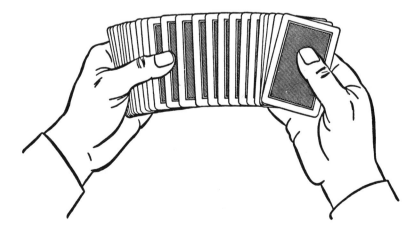

The Ribbon Spread

The deck is on the table. Position your right hand so that the index finger is on the left side of the pack. The thumb is on the inner end and the fingers are on top. Keeping the fingers in place, slide the entire pack to your right, gently lifting the index finger. The result is an even spread of cards across the table.

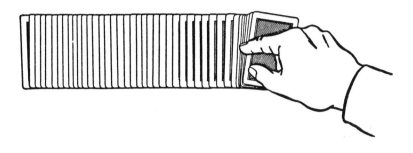

The Overhand Shuffle

The deck is held on its side in the left hand. The backs of the cards are facing the left thumb. The left thumb rests on the top card.

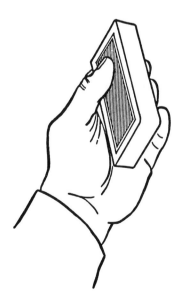

The right hand is cupped slightly as it takes the cards. The right thumb will almost touch the base of the left thumb. The right fingers hold the deck at the top. Lift the lower portion of the deck away with the right hand. The top half of the deck remains in the left hand.

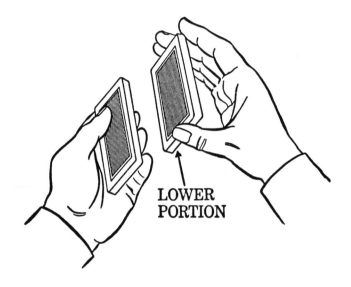

LOWER
PORTION

Bring the right-hand cards back over the left-hand stack. The left thumb now pulls some of the cards away from the right-hand pack. These cards will fall on those that are already in the left hand. The left hand comes up again and takes a few more cards with the thumb, pulling them in, and on top of the others. The right hand moves up and down slightly during this action until all the cards are now in the left hand.

The fingers of the left hand can help adjust any cards that are loosely held in the hand. This shuffle requires practice until you are comfortable using it. Here is how it can be used when doing your card magic.

Keeping Cards on the Bottom of the Deck

If you have cards on the bottom that must remain there, use your overhand shuffle. Instead of taking the bottom half away with the right hand, take the top section and continue to shuffle these until no cards are left in the right hand. The bottom cards will remain intact.

Keeping the Top Cards in Place

To do this you will repeat the moves just described, but you will turn your pack so that the cards face the left hand. In this way the top cards are on the bottom of the face-up pack and are controlled the same as bottom cards.

Bringing a Single Card to the Top

Let's say you have the bottom card, which is needed on top for the trick. Do the regular overhand shuffle. As you shuffle down to the end of the cards in the right hand, pull them off the deck singly. A bit of pressure between the thumb and fingers will bend the cards slightly to make it easier. The last card is dropped on top of the deck.

The Riffle Shuffle

Place the cards horizontally on the table in front of you. The right hand cuts the top section in half, placing the cards immediately to the right of the original pack. Your thumbs are behind the decks and your middle fingers are in front.

The index fingers lie lightly on top of each pack. The fingers of both hands almost touch where the two packs meet. Turn both packs so that they form a small "V" shape on the table.

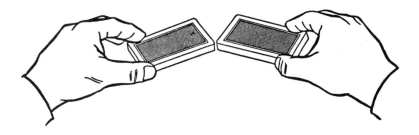

The right hand moves at an angle to the right, the left hand to the left. Press down on the decks with the index fingers, while the thumbs lift the cards off the table at the inner edges. Allow the cards to interlace as you relax pressure on the thumbs.

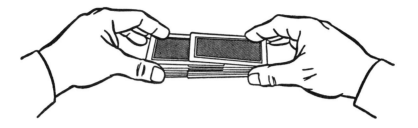

Push the two halves together and square the cards with your fingers.

Keeping the Top Stack in Place

The riffle shuffle is a natural for keeping a group of stacked cards in place while apparently shuffling. All you need do is control the shuffle so that when you come to the top cards they are held back as the left hand cards interlace beneath them. In other words you let *all* the left-hand cards fall before the last group in the right hand.

Control of Bottom Stack

At the onset of your shuffle, allow the left-hand cards to fall first—before you start to interlace them. This allows the bottom cards to remain in place.

Important! When performing tricks that require a stack on top, always shuffle the deck first, keeping the cards on top with the riffle. This eliminates the possibility of the cards being arranged . . . or so the spectator will believe.

Performing Your Magic

♠♣♥♦ The rules and "how-to" of doing magic.

Performing Your Magic

There is more to doing magic than just learning the tricks in this book. There are some rules that we have always felt are extremely important to the magician. We'll set them down here and hope that you will agree and follow some of this advice. Magic is a demanding art and requires a great deal of discipline.

1.   You should have a sincere love of magic and a desire to perform well. Never do magic for the sake of "showing off." In too many cases ego spoils a good performer and his or her performance. Don't be vain. Be humble and you'll go a lot further.

2. Magic needs people. If you like people, you'll have your rewards watching them enjoy themselves. You'll also make new and interesting friends.

3. Master your craft. Read, study and practice as often as you can. Try to make every performance technically perfect. Treat magic as one of the arts and strive for the perfection that will make you an artist.

4. Be very discriminating when selecting an effect for your repertoire. If a particular effect does not suit your style, forget it. Things must appear to happen by magic. Be natural and choose tricks that you can do easily, without straining. Try to vary your tricks to offer more versatility. Choose effects that will mystify, but above all, they should "ENTERTAIN!"

5. Try to vary your routining so that your act isn't top heavy with too many "take-a-card" tricks. Do your most powerful tricks and routines first. Once you have the audience with you, hit them with the simpler effects and end with a strong "blockbuster." Remember that you must not stay on too long. Magic musn't be tedious. Make every trick important. Always leave them wanting more.

6. Always make sure that your appearance is neat and you are well groomed. Your hands and fingernails should always be clean and manicured. Try to use a brand new deck of cards. A dirty deck will destroy the magic of your image. If you can afford it, give the deck away after your performance.

7. Be yourself. Don't try to emulate another's style or technique. Find your own style. If you can use humor in your act, do so. If it doesn't fit, don't try to be a comedian.

The serious magic student can turn professional and make money with his talent. The magic buff and collector can make friends with his hobby. We know of no more fulfilling and rewarding art form. It is truly **MAGIC!**

Bibliography

BENHAM, W. GURNEY. *Playing Cards,* Spring Books, London.

GARCIA, FRANK. *Million Dollar Card Secrets,* Million Dollar Productions, New York, 1972.

GARCIA, FRANK. *Super Subtle Card Miracles,* Million Dollar Productions, New York, 1973.

GARDNER, MARTIN. *Mathematics, Magic, and Mystery,* Dover Publishing, New York, 1956.

HILLIARD, JOHN NORTHERN. *Card Magic,* Carl W. Jones, Minneapolis, Minn., 1945.

HUGARD, JEAN. *Encyclopedia of Card Tricks,* Max Holden, New York, 1937.

THURSTON, HOWARD. *300 Tricks You Can Do,* Sandpiper Press, New York, 1927.

Index of Tricks

About the Authors

Frank Garcia and George Schindler have been friends and collaborators for more than 20 years. They operate The School for Magicians in New York City and are co-authors of *Amedeo's Continental Magic,* which was published in 1973.

FRANK GARCIA, author of *Million Dollar Card Tricks, Super Subtle Card Miracles,* and *Marked Cards and Loaded Dice,* recently published *All in a Nutshell,* a book that reveals the secret of the ancient "shell game," of which he is the undisputed master. Known as "the man with the million-dollar hands," Mr. Garcia has performed around the world before small groups, on the stage, and on television.

GEORGE SCHINDLER, who is known in the profession as the "Magicomedian," is the owner of Show-Biz Services, a company that supplies comedy materials to professional performers. His comedy magic has been featured in clubs and on the stage around the country. He is a lecturer and teacher of both magic and ventriloquism.